In warm, personal letters, followed by easy-to-understand recipes, ten girls from ten different countries share the adventure of learning to cook. Each girl contributes a meal of traditionally favorite dishes from her own country.

The beginning cook will be surprised to discover that once the basic techniques of cooking are learned, exciting foreign foods can easily be prepared with skill and flair, using ingredients that can readily be found in supermarkets and butcher stores.

Mildred O. Knopf's *Around the World Cookbook for Young People* is a joyous exploration of international recipes for new cooks of all ages.

Mildred O. Knopf's
Around the World Cookbook
for Young People

Illustrated by Gioia Fiammenghi

Alfred A. Knopf/New York

Mildred O. Knopf's
AROUND THE WORLD
COOKBOOK
FOR YOUNG PEOPLE

THIS IS A BORZOI BOOK PUBLISHED BY ALFRED A. KNOPF, INC.

Library of Congress Catalog Card Number: 66-13781

For
_____

Cathy
Vicky
Wendy E.
and for
Susan
with love

CONTENTS

4 / Katinaki of Greece

SOUPA AVEGOLEMONO
Chicken Soup with Egg and Lemon Sauce 55
HUNKAR BEGENDI / *Lamb Stew with Eggplant Purée 57*
RIZOGALO / *Rice Pudding with Cinnamon 60*
YIAOURTOPETA / *Yogurt Pie 62*

5 / Ella of the Netherlands

EIEREN GEVULD MET KAAS / *Eggs Stuffed with Cheese 71*
VARKENSCRIB / *Rolled Rib of Pork with Apples 72*
AARDAPPELPUREE / *Mashed Potatoes 75*
ROOM PUDDING / *Cream Pudding 77*

6 / Rosalina of Italy

STRACCIATELLA / *Chicken Broth with Beaten Egg 86*
RISOTTO ALLA MARINARA / *Rice with Seafood 87*
CIOCCOLATO ALLA CREMA / *Chocolate Cream 89*

7 / Shoko of Japan

CHAWAN-MUSHI
Steamed Broth with Chicken, Egg, and Vegetables 96
GOHAN / *Japanese-style Boiled Rice 99*
OYAKO-DOMBURI / *Rice with Chicken and Vegetables 100*
ICHIGO TO AWAYUKI / *Strawberries with Meringue 102*

Watch-outs and Warnings

* in recipe
Turn to glossary (pages 151 to 160)
for an explanation

To Inform You
From One Cook to Another

By and large, thanks to the bounties of nature, most countries of the world provide the same foods. Meats and fish, potatoes, rice, and starches, dairy products (milk, butter, cream, and cheese), vegetables, and fruit can be found almost anywhere. It is what the people of the world *do* with these products that makes "foreign" foods seem so different, so interesting and exciting. In this book, you will find an assortment of recipes that represent the native cooking of ten different countries. You will discover for yourself how fascinating it is to take the same food products we use and turn the basic ingredients into something entirely different from anything you have ever tasted. Using different combinations or new methods of preparation and of cooking, you will discover that you have stepped into the kitchens of other parts of the world! Before you know it, you will have become an accomplished cook of many foreign lands. So let us begin!

I know you can hardly wait to start cooking these fascinating dishes, but . . .

Cooking is like anything else you can't wait to do. You must know what you are doing before you start. It's like learning to play the piano, or how to swim, or how to ride a horse. So here are a few things you should know *before* beginning.

Getting Ready to Go to Market

Decide which recipe you want to try. Then read the list of ingredients at the top of the recipe. Now find out which of these things you already have in your refrigerator or cupboard. For instance, if the recipe calls for eggs and you have plenty of eggs you will not need to put eggs on your market list. But, if the recipe calls for butter and you have only a little dab left *that* means you must put butter on your list. So, study the list of ingredients very carefully, find out what you already have and what you do *not* have, complete your list, and off you go to market. *But don't forget your list.*

What to Wear in the Kitchen

Always remember to be sensible and don't go into the kitchen wearing a new or party dress. You must protect yourself when you are anywhere near fire or heat. Something like jeans or slacks or a simple cotton dress, covered by an apron, is the perfect costume for a cook.

Watch the Heat and Fire

Remember that fire and boiling water and other hot liquids are dangerous! You can easily be burned. If you're old enough to cook, you're old enough to be careful and old enough never to "fool around" when handling heated foods! This goes for everything that is HOT. For instance, never fill your pot *too* full when boiling water and, above all, never drop things like potatoes or onions into boiling water. *The splash they'll make will most likely be on you.* So, slide them in gently.

And when the time comes to take the pot off the stove, or the pan out of the oven, be *sure* to have mitts on your hands or two pot holders ready (one for each hand). This is very important.

Another thing, keep the handles of the pots pointing away from you so you won't bump them by mistake — they might tip over. And keep the handles away from the burners on the stove so they won't get hot. Everyone knows it's no fun being burned. I'm very, very serious because it is most important not to hurt yourself.

The Kitchen Must Be Clean

Before you start to cook, be sure your kitchen is clean — not just the pots and pans but the kitchen table or counter space where you plan to work and the breadboard, too, on which you're going to fix the food. And, above all, be certain *you* are clean . . . your hands and arms and even your face.

Getting Ready to Begin

When you return from marketing put everything the recipe calls for on the kitchen table. For example, if the recipe calls for 3 eggs, put 3 eggs on the table or counter space. In the case of eggs put them down carefully, preferably on a cloth to keep them from falling onto the floor and ending up like "Humpty Dumpty!"

Now read the list at the end of each recipe called *What You'll Need* to find out what bowls and beaters or pots and pans you're going to work with. Put everything within easy reach.

If you are going to serve as soon as you finish cooking and the recipe does not take more than about an hour to prepare, you might set the table before you start.

Now Begin!

Begin by reading the FIRST direction of the recipe carefully. Then do exactly what the direction tells you to do.

Next read the SECOND direction carefully and do what *it* says. Read the THIRD direction (not many of these recipes have more than three directions) and do what you're told to do. Then the job's completed! Easier than you thought, wasn't it?

Pay Attention While You Work

If you start something . . . finish it! Food costs money as well as being important to your health. So don't waste it by losing interest and letting your unfinished effort stand around until it spoils! If you start something, stay with it and don't get impatient if it takes a little longer to complete than you think it should. Remember how good it's going to taste!

Pay special attention when something's cooking on top of the stove or in the oven and, for goodness sake, don't leave the kitchen to telephone your friends! No time now for nice long chats. Should your girl friend call you when you're in the middle of things, tell her you'll call her back. As a matter of fact, if you have a minute between things, that's the best time to tidy up!

Tidying Up

You must allow yourself plenty of room to work in, so *clean up as you go along.* Measuring cups and spoons and other utensils that are to be used more than once in a recipe should be thoroughly rinsed before being reused. You'll always find a moment while you're waiting for something to finish cooking. For instance, when you have a roast or cake in the oven that won't be ready for a while, TIDY UP! Grab those pots and bowls and pans, measuring cups and stirring spoons, and dump them in the sink. Attack them with plenty of warm water, Mother's detergent, a sponge, and a scrubbing pad! Pretend it's a game and see how quickly it can be done. Remember, a good cook is always proud of a clean kitchen. So pick up, wash up, don't pile up . . . please!

Your Bright Reward

Now there's nothing left to do but invite your family and your friends to dinner! I'll let you in on a very special secret: the greatest fun is when *they* sit down to eat what *you've* prepared and *they* can't believe you cooked it by yourself! Don't be shy when you receive their praise. *You'll* know you've earned it. And indeed you have.

Good luck and love,
Mildred O. Knopf

·1·
TOVE
OF DENMARK

God Morgen:

What a wonderful time I've had this week! I only wish everybody could be this happy! But I guess *Moder* is right. She says I *must* speak slowly when I'm telling something, otherwise I'll not be understood. So I'll try to write to you slowly.

My name is Tove and I live in the city of Copenhagen, the capital of Denmark. Copenhagen is a beautiful city with a river running through. It has parks and big hotels and restaurants and a Royal Palace where our King and Queen live. I live with Moder and *Fader* and my three older brothers, Erik, Lars, and Sven. My brothers are only interested in girls and cars. I'm a girl but they're not interested in me. They just chase me up and down the stairs and try to catch my braids, and they tell each other secrets but they never let me hear!

Fader is a doctor. He works hard to make people well, and my moder takes good care of the family. She is also very clever and makes embroidered things like cross-stitch flowers on pillow cases, and birds and cows and little trees on tablecloths. I suppose I will learn to embroider, too, but right now I can only think about what I learned this week! It began last Thursday when my cousin Margrete came to visit us. Margrete's a lot of fun and laughs at anything I say. I wish she were my sister, but she's grown-up and she's getting married very soon. That's why she came to Copenhagen to ask Moder to help her buy her clothes.

Margrete lives in Odense which is on the island of Fyn across the water from Copenhagen. Odense is where Hans Christian Andersen was born. He is a famous Danish author who was very poor when he was young. He was unhappy for a long, long time because no one read what he wrote, but later, when he wrote fairy tales, he became famous everywhere. Of course you've read THE UGLY DUCKLING, THE BRAVE TIN SOLDIER, THE LITTLE MERMAID, and THE RED SHOES. Aren't they lovely stories?

Margrete's moder is Aunt Anna. She's my moder's sister and is busy all the time because she has an inn at Odense where she cooks and cooks and cooks for the tourists who visit Hans Christian Andersen's house. Margrete has always helped Aunt Anna in the kitchen, but she's much too busy now getting ready for her wedding. She asked Moder if she could take me back to help Aunt Anna cook. Moder said I could go because it was my spring holiday, and just watching Aunt Anna in her kitchen should make a first-rate cook of me!

So, next day Margrete gathered together all her boxes of new clothes and we started for Odense. We drove into the country past little farms and miles of lilac hedges growing on both sides of the road. The land in Denmark is very, very flat so the farmers have planted lilac hedges (which are very high) to keep the wind from sweeping across the fields and blowing at the farmland. When we drove across the island to get the ferry to Odense, the lilacs were in bloom. How good they smelled! The air was perfumed all the way to the far side of the island. When we got there Margrete drove the car onto the ferry. It's especially built to carry cars. We parked and climbed up the stairs to the restaurant. As soon as the ferryboat began to move everyone began to eat. What a delicious *Smørrebrød!* Do you know that *Smørre* means butter and *brød* means bread? In Denmark we make sandwiches on one piece of buttered bread. We pile on all sorts of things like cold roast beef with pickle slices and grated horseradish; liver paste with chopped bacon; smoked salmon with minced dill and lemon slices; sliced hard-boiled eggs with anchovy fillets; sardines with scrambled eggs; or ham with mustard and radishes on top. Margrete says when you make sandwiches like these, you must use plenty of sweet butter on bread that's very fresh. And you should be sure to make the sandwiches look pretty. I'm going to surprise the family and make lots and lots of these.

When we reached Aunt Anna's inn, it was very crowded. As soon as the people left the ferry, they hurried there. Aunt Anna kissed my cheek and said, "So you've come to help your busy aunt? I'm very glad. You can start right away."

She tied a big white apron around my waist. "Start making a macaroni *salat*. Cut up the ham and the cucumber pickles, and make a sauce with sour cream and mayonnaise and seasonings. Here, it's written down for you. And remember it's important to follow the directions carefully.

When you're through, tell me and I'll show you how to mix the *frikedeller*. This is a busy day, so hurry, little Tove."

What fun! What fun! Aunt Anna's kitchen was the busiest place I've ever seen. I wish you could know how much I enjoyed myself. Aunt Anna says you're sure to enjoy cooking if you love to eat. Especially the country food of Denmark. I'm sure that's true because I got hungrier all the time.

When I'm back in Copenhagen (I wish I didn't have to go so soon!), I'll say to Moder, "Take your embroidery and please sit in the living room. I am going to the kitchen. Then you can see what I've learned." I think she'll be surprised, don't you?

Farvel,
Tove

Macaroni Salat

MACARONI SALAD

Serves 12

4 quarts water
1 teaspoon salt
½ pound small-size elbow macaroni
4 eggs
1 teaspoon dry mustard
1 cup mayonnaise (½ pint jar)
1 cup sour cream (½ pint carton)
½ teaspoon salt
¼ teaspoon ground, black pepper
½ pound pre-cooked ham
1 cup cucumber-pickle slices (15-ounce jar)
2-ounce jar chopped pimientos
1 tablespoon dried dill

FIRST:

This salad is best made a day ahead as it must be served very cold. To begin, put 4 quarts of water in a large pot, add 1 teaspoon of salt, turn the heat high, and bring to a rolling boil.* When the water boils, gradually add ½ pound of small-size elbow macaroni. Do *not* add it all at once or the water will stop boiling. Boil for 12 minutes, occasionally stirring* the bottom of the pot with a large spoon (preferably wooden so as not to cut up the macaroni) so the macaroni does not stick. When the macaroni is tender, put a colander in the sink and carry the pot to the sink, using 2 pot holders on the handles. Be sure to use great care. The pot is very hot! Carefully and slowly pour the macaroni into the colander and let it drain. (If any has stuck to the bottom of the pot, you may scrape it out.) Run cold water from the tap through the macaroni to help cool it and to remove excess starch so it will not stick together. When it is thoroughly drained, put the macaroni in a large mixing bowl. The bowl must be very, *very* large so the macaroni is not pressed together into one big lump. When it is cool enough to handle, plunge your hands (be sure they are freshly washed) into it and turn it over and over. This will keep it separated. Be sure to do this several times.

SECOND: *To Hard-Boil Eggs*

While the macaroni is cooling, put 4 eggs in a small pot, cover with cold water, and bring to a full boil. Boil for 10 minutes. Remove the pot to the sink and pour off all the water. Fill the pot with cold water. Five minutes later pour off all the water and fill the pot again with fresh cold water. Five minutes later remove the eggs and peel.* Dry the peeled eggs in a clean kitchen towel and let them cool to room temperature.* Separate the hard-boiled yolks from the whites by slicing the eggs in half lengthwise and using a small fork to remove the yolks. (You are not going to use the whites in this recipe. They may be used by chopping them for a salad, or stuffing them with mashed tuna fish mixed with mayonnaise.) When the yolks are cool, put them in a medium-size mixing bowl and mash them with the fork until no lumps remain. Add 1 teaspoon of dry mustard and mix well so no mustard lumps remain. Then slowly stir in 1 cup of mayonnaise and 1 cup of sour cream. Season with ½ teaspoon of salt and ¼ teaspoon of pepper, and pour this dressing on top of the cool macaroni. No matter how sticky it may seem, turn the dressing into the macaroni with your bare hands, over and over. This is fun even though it is messy!

THIRD:

Wash your hands to clean off the sauce. Now cut ½ pound of pre-cooked ham and 1 cup of cucumber-pickle slices into tiny, bite-size pieces. Chop the pimiento into very small pieces and add it with the ham and cucumber-pickle and 1 tablespoon dried dill to the macaroni. Mix with your hands as you did before. When everything is thoroughly mixed, wash your hands again. Cover the bowl with wax paper or clear plastic paper and refrigerate for several hours, or preferably overnight. When ready to serve, put the macaroni salad on a serving platter that has been chilled in the icebox for 15 minutes. Serve very cold.

WHAT YOU'LL NEED:

large pot

measuring spoons

large stirring spoon
    (preferably wooden)

colander

2 pot holders

very large mixing bowl

small pot for eggs

clean kitchen towel

medium mixing bowl

small fork

small kitchen knife

wax paper or clear plastic
    paper

platter

serving spoon

Frikedeller

MEAT BALLS

Serves 6

½ pound ground raw veal
½ pound ground raw pork
2 tablespoons flour
½ cup finely grated bread crumbs (see note)
1¼ cups milk
1 egg (slightly beaten)
½ teaspoon salt
¼ teaspoon ground, black pepper
1 teaspoon dried dill
1 medium onion, finely grated (approximately 3 inches wide)
butter (several sticks)
½ cup flour
finely chopped fresh parsley

FIRST:

Ask your butcher to put ½ pound raw veal and ½ pound raw pork through his meat chopper twice. Buy your meat the day you plan to use it — chopped meat tastes best when freshly ground. When you make the meat balls, put both these meats into a good-size mixing bowl and add 2 tablespoons of flour and ½ cup of finely grated bread crumbs. Mix well with a spoon, then add 1¼ cups milk, 1 slightly beaten egg, ½ teaspoon salt, ¼ teaspoon pepper, 1 teaspoon dried dill. Beat* well with spoon. Peel* 1 medium onion and grate* on a fine grater. (Careful of your knuckles.) Add the grated onion to the bowl. Mix well. Cover the bowl with plastic or wax paper and put it in the refrigerator to chill for 1 hour or more. The mixture will thicken as it chills and be much easier to handle. If you like, it may be prepared early in the day.

SECOND:

About half an hour before dinner, start to prepare. Preheat oven* to 200°. Melt* 2 ounces (½ stick) of butter in a *large* frying pan over medium heat. Once the butter is melted, remove the pan from the heat so the butter doesn't burn. Take the mixture out of the refrigerator. Put ½ cup of flour on a breadboard and smooth it out. Rub the palms of your hands with the flour, scoop out a heaping tablespoon of meat, and shape it lightly with your hands into a 2-inch ball. As you shape each ball, put it in the pan until the pan is almost full. The meat balls will brown much better if the pan is *not too full*. Put the pan back on the heat and brown the meat balls first on one side, then on the other. When you turn them, do it gently with a tablespoon as this particular type of meat ball is very light and tender. When they are brown all through (no pink showing!), remove from the pan with a large slotted spoon and put them on a platter. Put the platter in a preheated 200° oven to keep the meat balls warm while you prepare the others. Repeat by melting another 2 ounces (½ stick) of butter in the pan and continuing to shape and fry the other meat balls. This recipe should make approximately 2 dozen meat balls.

THIRD:

When all the meat balls are made, take 2 pot holders to remove the serving platter from the oven. Pour the remaining butter over them and sprinkle generously with finely chopped parsley. Serve with mashed potatoes (see page 75) and with pickled beets. The Danes often serve red cabbage, but any vegetable you prefer will do.

Note: Bread crumbs may be bought at bakeries and at supermarkets, but the best ones are those you make yourself. Homemade bread crumbs are easily made. Save all your stale, leftover bread, put it on a cookie sheet in a preheated 250° oven, and leave it until it is quite crisp and dry. It is impossible to tell you exactly how long the bread must be kept in the oven because it depends on the age and the thickness of the bread. In any case, turn the bread once while it is drying out. If you have a blendor you have nothing to worry about. Simply break the dry bread into pieces, put six or seven pieces in the blendor at the same time, turn the blendor on to *low* and, magically, there you have it . . . bread crumbs! If you do not have a blendor, put the dried bread pieces on a board and roll them out with a rolling pin. If you want extra-fine crumbs, shake them through a fine mesh strainer.

WHAT YOU'LL NEED:

good-size mixing bowl	large frying pan
measuring spoons	breadboard
measuring cup	tablespoon
wooden mixing spoon	large slotted spoon
fine grater	platter
plastic or wax paper	2 pot holders

Arme Riddere

POOR KNIGHTS

Serves 4

1 box frozen raspberries (thawed)
8 slices white bread
1 cup milk
6 tablespoons sugar
1½ teaspoons cinnamon
¼ pound butter (1 stick)

FIRST:

Prepare a raspberry sauce by putting the contents of 1 thawed box of frozen raspberries into the electric blendor and turning it on for a moment. There, you have the sauce! Set a good-size strainer over a bowl and pour the liquid through the strainer. Rub with a spoon until all the liquid has gone through and there are only seeds left in the strainer to throw away. If you have no electric blendor, the raspberries may be put directly into the strainer and worked through with a spoon into the bowl. The sauce must be ready to use as soon as the dessert is ready. To make strawberry sauce instead of raspberry see note 2, on following page.

SECOND:

Dry 8 slices of white bread (see note 1). Put the dried bread on a baking sheet or breadboard to keep it flat. Spoon 2 tablespoons of milk all over each slice, then sprinkle all 8 slices evenly, first with 6 tablespoons of sugar, then with 1½ teaspoons of cinnamon.

THIRD:

Turn the oven to 200°. Melt* *half* the butter in your largest frying pan. Use a broad spatula to gently lift up as many slices of bread as the pan will hold. Fry them over medium heat, first on unsugared side, then on sugared side, until they are all nicely browned. Place them on a serving platter, sugared sides up, and put the platter in a preheated 200° oven* to keep them warm until you have browned the remaining slices.

FOURTH:

Warm the sauce in a pot. Not too hot, mind you, just warm. Warm* a sauce boat or bowl, put the sauce in, and serve immediately with the Arme Riddere. Serve two slices on each dessert plate, and be sure the plates are warm. Very delicious!

Note 1:   To dry bread
Place the required number of bread slices on a baking sheet. Put the baking sheet in a preheated 150° oven. After 15 minutes, turn the slices and leave them in the oven for 15 minutes more. When ready they should feel dry but not brown.

Note 2:   To prepare strawberry sauce
Simply substitute a box of thawed strawberries for the raspberries and proceed as for raspberry sauce (page 21). Strawberry seeds being so tiny, it will not be necessary to run the strawberry sauce through a strainer unless you have no blendor.

WHAT YOU'LL NEED:

electric blendor
good-size strainer
spoon (preferably wooden)
baking sheet
measuring cup
measuring spoons

largest frying pan
broad spatula or cake turner
serving platter
pot
sauce boat or bowl
individual serving plates

·2·
DEBORAH
OF ENGLAND

How do you do:

My name is Deborah. I live in England and our house is in a lovely part of London called St. John's Wood. Mummy and Daddy and my two Corgi dogs live with me. The Corgis are named Jack and Jill and are my best friends, except for Nanny whose real name is Miss Elsie Jean Campbell, although no one calls her anything but Nanny. Nanny comes from Scotland and she's been my companion from the time that I was three. Sometimes, I suppose, people think I'm lonely because I'm an only child, but of course that is very silly because I have Jack and Jill and Nanny, who takes me to Scotland whenever she can.

The houses in St. John's Wood have beautiful gardens. But Mummy's garden is the loveliest of all. Especially when it's spring and the rhodos (I expect *you* call them rhododendrons), the azaleas, the lilies of the valley, the many-colored lupins, and tall white lilacs are in bloom. They are every bit as gorgeous as the ones at the Chelsea Flower Show *which is probably the most beautiful flower show anyone can see!*

Mummy and Daddy give a lot of parties and when they do, it's fun to watch Cook (whose name is Mrs. Jones) prepare for Mummy's guests. But I'm afraid she doesn't like to have me in the kitchen, for when I say I'd be pleased to help, she says she can't permit a young lady to do anything like that. Don't you think that is silly? It will be years and years before I am grown-up! I do wish Cook could understand how much I would enjoy helping her.

Last summer, Nanny took me to visit her sister's farm in Scotland while Mummy and Daddy were on holiday with friends. Well, Nanny has a charming sister whose name is Mrs. Gordon James MacGregor, but whose first name is Alice. She lives with her husband and two children on a farm near Glasgow. They have cows and chickens, dogs and sheep, and everyone is very nice. The very best thing I like about the MacGregors is that they all eat together in a big kitchen and, when they're not eating, they're laughing all the time!

Cook will *not* believe I learned to cook such delicious things last summer. She will *not* listen when I tell her I already know a great deal about cooking! She will *not* let me show her, so I'm afraid I shall have to wait until next summer to start to cook again.

Nanny says that when Mummy and Daddy go on holiday to the south of France this summer, she will ask me to her sister's farm again. And this time, Mrs. MacGregor has promised to show me how to make Finnan Haddie and Gooseberry Fool and other exciting things! Though I must admit, I can't imagine anything more exciting than the things I learned last year. Nanny said I did *verra guid* for a *wee lass o' nine* (that's how they speak in Scotland). But now I'm ten and I shall do better still, and I won't

have to ask so many silly questions. I should love to invite
you to the MacGregor farm. *You* would believe (even if
Cook does not) that I *can* truly cook. This is what I learned
last year: Cock-a-Leekie Soup, Toad-in-the-Hole, and
Bread and Raisin Pudding. Would *you* like to try these
things yourself? I'll tell you how they're done.

Good-by from Jack and Jill and me,
Deborah

Cock-a-Leekie Soup
Best prepared the day before / Serves 8

1 3-pound frying chicken (cut up by joints)
salt
pepper
¼ pound butter (1 stick)
6 leeks
½ teaspoon dried thyme
1 cup parsley tops (short stems)
4 14-ounce cans clear, unconcentrated chicken broth
2 cups water
1 teaspoon salt
½ teaspoon ground, black pepper

FIRST:

Ask your butcher to cut up 1 3-pound frying chicken. He will cut it by joints — wings, legs, thighs, breasts, etc. Put the pieces on a breadboard and sprinkle both sides of the pieces with salt and pepper. Melt* ¼ pound butter (1 stick) in a large, deep frying pan. Spear the chicken pieces, one at a time, with a long-handled fork and put them in the hot butter. Let them sizzle and brown over high flame, first on one side, then on the other, until they are appetizingly brown on *both* sides. Be careful that the hot butter does not spatter on you. It can hurt!

SECOND:

Cut the green "tails" off 6 leeks and throw them away. Now, carefully slice the white ends of the leeks crosswise into circles with a vegetable knife. Put them in a colander and run cold water through them. Leeks, like celery, must be washed as they usually have bits of dirt inside their stalks. Let the water drain off. While they are draining, take your long-handled fork and remove all the pieces of chicken from the frying pan to a large, roomy soup pot. (It is important to have the pot really roomy.) When the pan is empty, put the sliced leeks into the butter in which the chicken was fried and cook them lightly (that means do rlot have the flame too high) until they are no longer crisp, but do not let them brown. Use a rubber spatula to scrape *all* the remaining butter and the leeks into the soup pot with the chicken. Be sure you have the frying pan *clean!* Sprinkle with ½ tea-spoon dried thyme and add 1 cup of parsley tops tied together with a piece of twine. The parsley is put in this way to make it easier to remove when the soup is done. Pour the contents of 4 14-ounce cans of clear, unconcentrated chicken broth and 2 cups of water into the pot. Add 1 teaspoon of salt and ½ teaspoon of pepper, turn the heat to high, and bring the soup to a boil,* then turn the heat down to a simmer.* Continue to simmer for 1 hour. Turn the heat off, lift the soup pot off with 2 pot holders, and allow the soup to cool to room temperature.* This will take sev-eral hours depending on the temperature of the kitchen.

THIRD:

After the soup is cool, remove the bunch of parsley and throw it away. Use a slotted spoon so that the soup will drain away from each piece of chicken, and remove all the chicken from the soup to the breadboard. Take a paring knife and pull the skin off the chicken meat. Take the meat off the bones (be careful not to include any gristle or tiny bones). Cut the meat into bite-size pieces and put them back in the pot. Put the soup (be sure it is cool) into the refrigerator and leave it overnight. This is impor-tant and I'll tell you why. The fat will rise to the top and turn hard. When it is hard, it is extremely easy to remove every bit with a metal spoon. (Don't throw it away. It may be kept in a little jar in the refrigerator and is excellent for frying.) This soup is very, very good. Even better after twenty-four hours.

WHAT YOU'LL NEED:

breadboard	measuring spoons
large, deep frying pan	measuring cup
long-handled fork	small piece of twine
vegetable cutting knife	2 pot holders
colander	slotted spoon
large soup pot	paring knife
rubber spatula	metal spoon

Toad-in-the-Hole
Preheat oven* to 450° / Serves 4 to 5

¾ cup flour
¼ teaspoon salt
1 egg
1 cup milk
2 tablespoons butter (¼ stick)
1 pound skinless frankfurters

FIRST:

Before starting, turn the oven up to 450°. Put ¾ cup flour into a small mixing bowl. Add ¼ teaspoon salt, break 1 egg* into the bowl, and pour in 1 cup of milk. Use a whisk or rotary egg beater and beat* the batter until very smooth. No lumps, please. No lumps at all. Set it aside and let it rest about 20 minutes.

SECOND:

Melt* 1 tablespoon of butter in a large frying pan. Put 1 pound skinless frankfurters into the butter and brown them lightly, first on one side, then on the other. Turn off the heat.

THIRD:

Put 1 tablespoon butter in an 8 x 12 oven-proof glass dish. Put the dish on the center rack of the preheated oven until the butter melts. But watch out, the butter must not burn! Use 2 pot holders to remove the dish from the oven. Put the frankfurters (one alongside the other) into the heated dish. Be careful not to burn your fingers. Give the batter in the bowl a short beating to be certain it is smooth and pour it over the frankfurters. Use a rubber spatula or tablespoon to scrape the bowl so every bit is used. Pop the dish back into the oven and leave it there for 30 minutes or until the batter is baked a crusty brown. Remember to use pot holders when you remove the dish from the oven! Warm* the plates. You may serve this with your favorite mustard and with any green vegetable that suits you best.

WHAT YOU'LL NEED:

measuring cup

measuring spoons

small mixing bowl

whisk or egg beater

large frying pan

8 x 12 oven-proof glass baking dish

2 pot holders

rubber spatula or tablespoon

individual serving plates

Bread and Raisin Pudding
Preheat oven* to 375° / Serves 6

8 slices dried white bread
  (see note page 22)
3 eggs
½ cup sugar
2 cups milk
¼ teaspoon salt
1 teaspoon vanilla extract
¼ teaspoon ground nutmeg
1 teaspoon butter (leave out of refrigerator to soften)
¼ cup seedless raisins
2 teaspoons slivered almonds (skinned)
1 cup currant jelly or applesauce (optional)
2 tablespoons hot water (optional)

FIRST:

Turn the oven on and heat to 375°. Put 8 slices of dried white
bread (leave the crusts on) on a breadboard. Take a bread knife
and cut each slice 4 times down then 4 times across. This should
give you a quart of bread cubes.

SECOND:

Use a whisk or rotary-type egg beater to beat* 3 eggs with ½
cup of sugar in a good-size mixing bowl until light and smooth.
Pour 2 cups of milk into the eggs, add ¼ teaspoon of salt, and
beat until everything is thoroughly mixed. Stir in 1 teaspoon of
vanilla extract and ¼ teaspoon of ground nutmeg.

THIRD:

Grease* a 2-quart glass casserole or other oven-proof dish with 1 teaspoon soft butter. Put the bread cubes into this, pour the contents of the bowl on top, scraping the bowl carefully with a rubber spatula or tablespoon. Gently, stir everything with a spoon. Add ¼ cup of washed, seedless raisins and 2 teaspoons of slivered almonds, which can be bought in small packages in food stores. Place the casserole on the center rack of the pre-heated 375° oven and bake for half an hour. When the pudding is baked, use 2 pot holders to carry the casserole from the oven. Let it cool to room temperature.* Do not refrigerate. Serve with melted currant jelly or with applesauce.

Melted jelly:
Put 1 cup of currant jelly in a small pot. Turn the heat to medium and stir with a small fork until the jelly melts. Add 2 tablespoons hot water and stir until combined. Let it cool, then pour it into a sauce boat or pitcher. A word of warning: never pour boiling liquid into a glass or china container. This is dangerous as the container may crack or break easily when filled with boiling liquid.

WHAT YOU'LL NEED:

breadboard	2-quart oven-proof casserole
baking sheet	rubber spatula or tablespoon
bread knife	stirring spoon
good-size mixing bowl	2 pot holders
whisk or egg beater	small pot
measuring cup	small fork
measuring spoons	sauce boat or pitcher
small piece paper towel	6 small serving bowls

·3·
MARIANNE
OF FRANCE

Bonjour:

My name is Marianne. My home is in Paris near the Eiffel Tower, although right now I am not living there and I must tell you why. My *papa* is a lawyer and he went on a most important business trip and my *maman* went along. I am spending all summer with my dear *grandmère* at Anglet, a little town in the Basque country close to Les Pyrénees Mountains and to Spain. It is very beautiful. The people here speak French but also Basque which is a very old language. Some of the Basque words are the same as Japanese but nobody can tell you why.

I love to visit Grandmère's house. It is warm and comfortable during the cold winter weather, yet very cool in summer when the green shutters are closed against the sun. Best of all, I like the kitchen with the copper pots and pans hanging from the walls. I do not like our Paris kitchen where everything is aluminum and stainless steel. In Grandmère's garden there are fruits and vegetables. Row after row of baby carrots, tiny peas, small string beans, and many heads of lettuce. Grandmère insists that vegetables must be picked when they are very young. I have promised to remember that young vegetables are best. Her fruit trees are mostly pears and apples. Their branches are tied to straight lines of heavy wire so they cannot break, not even when the wind blows from the sea. The pears and apples on their straight branches hang like ornaments from a Christmas tree. How impatiently I have waited for them to ripen! Now, *enfin!* the pears are ripe, the arms of the trees against the heavy wires are *plein*, plein, plein (you would say full, full, full)! It has been a lovely summer, especially since I've shared a secret with Grandmère.

It began the morning we drove to the *Grand Marché*, the great public market at Biarritz, a most fashionable town not far from small Anglet. The market is inside a huge building and is lined on both sides and down the middle with crowded little stalls. Some of these have vegetables and fruit; others are full of country sausages, hanging down in strings; some have eggs and cheese and tremendous blocks of butter shaped like the hat *Monsieur*, our mayor, wears on important holidays. It is astonishing to watch *Madame*, the butter lady, cut the butter block with a long, strong wire. She never mistakes the amount you want, even by a gram! Still other stalls have chickens, ducks, and pigeons, and the butcher sells lamb and veal and beef. But the loveliest are the flower stalls with carnations, roses, dahlias, and zinnias. They are *magnifique!* There is even a smaller building where shellfish and fresh fish are sold. If you could only see the lobsters! They are actually alive, crawling over seaweed and waving their feelers in the air.

My secret started when I said, "Oh, Grandmère, it is all so fresh and lovely! One could wish to eat it all! May I choose?"

And Grandmère said, "Of course, *petite*. How would you like to cook the dinner?"

"But Grandmère, I have never learned to cook," I said.

"*Bien*, it is time. Your maman will be so pleased."

And that's how my secret for Maman began.

I chose to make an onion soup because that is Papa's favorite. He has told me that he and Maman often ate it when they were very young and first engaged to be married. They would go in the middle of the night to the Paris *Halles* (the central market) and eat the most delicious onion soup with melted cheese on crusty bread floating on top.

I shall always remember the first day I learned to cook. The onion soup, the roasted chicken, and Grandmère's pears, gently poached and served with a chocolate sauce! Grandmère boiled some new potatoes and, having removed their jackets, browned them in butter. And when we sat down to eat, Grandmère said she was proud of me. Now I was a *cuisinière* . . . a cook. It made me feel so important.

Au revoir,
Marianne

Soupe à l'Oignon

ONION SOUP

Serves 8

5 good-size onions (4 to 5 inches across)
4 tablespoons butter (½ stick)
1 tablespoon olive oil
1 heaping teaspoon flour
3 cans beef consommé (concentrate)
2 cups water
1 teaspoon salt
½ teaspoon ground, black pepper
6 slices white bread (French bread preferred)
butter
finely grated Parmesan cheese (may be bought in a package)

FIRST:

Put 5 good-size onions on a breadboard. Peel* the skins off the onions with a paring knife, then slice them across carefully into rings (about ¼ inch) with a larger slicing knife. You might put a paper towel under the onions so they will not slip on the board as you cut. Hold one onion at a time firmly with your left hand while slicing with your right. When you have a job like this to do, never, never hurry. Take your time to avoid accidents. Separate the rings with your fingers.

SECOND:

Melt* 4 tablespoons of butter in a large frying pan. Add 1 tablespoon of olive oil. Add the onions and let them cook until they turn gold in color. Stir* now and then, turning the onion rings with a large spoon. Cook the onions until they are limp and colored dark tan evenly on both sides. When they have changed color, sprinkle them with 1 heaping teaspoon of flour, being careful that the flour goes on evenly all over the onions. Tilt the spoon slightly as you hold it in your hand, tap your index finger against the spoon as you move it slowly above the contents of the pot. You do not want the flour to fall in one place and form a lump. Then stir the flour into the onions and continue to cook for another 5 minutes.

THIRD:

Transfer the onions to a good-size pot and scrape the pan with a rubber spatula or tablespoon so you don't waste any of the browned butter. Put 3 cans of beef consommé (concentrate) and 2 cups of water into the pot, add 1 teaspoon of salt and ½ teaspoon of pepper. Place the cover on the pot, bring it to a boil.* Stir just once to be sure nothing is sticking to the bottom of the pot, then turn down the heat and allow the soup to simmer* for 20 minutes.

FOURTH:

Preheat the oven* to 375°. Cut six ¾ inch thick rounds of white bread (by placing an inverted glass on the bread and pressing down with a twisting motion) or, preferably, cut six 1-inch-thick slices of French bread (crusty French bread is best because it doesn't go to pieces in the soup). Place the bread slices on a cookie sheet or large, shallow baking pan and toast in the oven, first on one side then on the other, until nicely browned. The timing will depend on how fresh the bread is and how brown you like the bread. Remove from the oven with a pot holder (leave the heat on), butter the toast, and sprinkle the pieces generously with finely grated Parmesan cheese. Return to the oven, but only long enough to melt the cheese. Warm* the soup plates. With a slotted spoon, put a large spoonful of onions in each heated soup plate, then take a ladle and transfer the broth into the plates until they are nearly full. Float a piece of prepared toast on top of each, and serve as quickly as possible. This is the most famous of all French soups.

WHAT YOU'LL NEED:

breadboard
paper towel
paring knife
slicing knife
measuring spoons
large frying pan
large stirring spoon
good-size pot with cover
rubber spatula or tablespoon
measuring cup

water glass
cookie sheet or large, shallow
    baking pan
2 pot holders
butter knife
slotted spoon
ladle
soup plates or
    individual soup bowls

Poulet Rôti

ROASTED CHICKEN

Preheat oven* to 450° / Serves 4

1 3-to-3½ pound chicken
salt
ground, black pepper

1 large onion (4 to 5 inches across)
¼ pound butter (1 stick) (leave out to soften)
1 14-ounce can clear, unconcentrated chicken broth
1 small bunch watercress or parsley tops

FIRST:

Remember, when buying a chicken, to choose one that shows a lot
of yellow color underneath the skin. This means the chicken is fat
and will be juicy and have a lot more flavor when done. Cooking,
you know, is only half the job. Shopping at the market is important, too. Before starting to cook, turn the oven on to 450°. Stand
the chicken on its neck and hold it with your left hand while you
shake approximately 1 teaspoon of salt and ⅛ teaspoon of pepper inside the chicken with your right hand. Peel* a large onion
with a paring knife, cut it into quarters, and put it inside the bird.
Take a pointed skewer and pin the opening together. Cut a piece
of string about twelve inches long. Tie it first around the tail end
of the chicken and make a knot, then wrap it around the legs
and tie them down to the tail. This will keep the legs in place
when the chicken is in the oven. It will also give it a tidier look
when it is served. Finally, tuck the wing tips under the chicken to
keep the wings close to the body.

SECOND:

Smear the bird thickly with ¼ pound soft butter. Use plenty and
do not be afraid to do this with your hands. But be sure they are
clean! Generously sprinkle the entire surface of the buttered
chicken with salt and pepper, then lift it up and put it in a shallow baking pan. Do not use a pan with high sides (no higher than
two inches) since that would keep the heat from browning the
bird all over. Place the pan on the center rack of the preheated
450° oven. Put the contents of a 14-ounce can of clear, unconcentrated chicken broth into a pot and heat but do not boil. Keep

on the lowest heat, and when the chicken begins to take on a nice brown color (after about 20 minutes) begin to baste.* After basting, roast for another 10 minutes, then baste again. At the end of 30 or 40 minutes, the chicken should be nicely browned. Turn the oven down to 375° and continue to baste every 10 minutes with additional broth until there is enough liquid in the bottom of the pan to use for basting. When that happens, you will not need to add any more liquid, just use the liquid in the pan. A 3- to 3½-pound chicken should not take more than an hour or hour-and-a-quarter to be roasted through.

THIRD:

Just before serving, turn off the oven heat. Remove the roasting pan from the oven (remember those pot holders!) and set it on the counter or kitchen table. Take kitchen scissors and cut the string around the legs, give the string a little pull, remove it, and throw it away. Put the chicken on a serving platter and return it to the oven (you did turn off the oven heat, didn't you?), leave the oven door open, and now prepare the gravy.

To prepare the gravy:

With 2 pot holders pick up the pan (it is still hot!), put it on top of the stove, turn the heat to high, and let the juices in the pan begin to boil* — but watch out for splattering! While they boil, scrape the bits that are stuck to the bottom of the pan (they make the best gravy) with a wooden spoon or rubber scraper and stir them into the liquid. Warm* a gravy boat or bowl and put it on the table with a sieve on top. Carefully pick up the pan with 2 pot holders and pour all the juices through the sieve. Now you are ready to serve your delicious bird. Remove the platter from the oven, and decorate* it around the edge with a small bunch of watercress or parsley tops. Watercress is particularly delicious when mixed up on your dinner plate with the *jus* or gravy. *Bon appetit!*

measuring spoons

paring knife

pointed skewer

string (12 inches long)

shallow baking pan

medium-size pot

large kitchen spoon or
 basting bulb

2 pot holders

kitchen scissors

serving platter

wooden spoon or rubber scraper

gravy boat or bowl

sieve

Les Poires Pochées, Grandmère

GRANDMOTHER'S STEWED PEARS

Best prepared the day before / Serves 4

2 cups water

1 cup sugar

4 large pears (good-size Bartlett pears preferred)

few drops vanilla extract

Chocolate Sauce (see page 47)

FIRST:

Put 2 cups of water and 1 cup of sugar in a large pot. Turn the flame to high. Stir* until the sugar melts, then let the syrup come to a boil.* While waiting, take a paring knife and skin 4 large pears. Do not cut too deeply, just remove the skins and be sure to *leave the stems on.* They look so much prettier that way. As each pear is peeled* put it on a plate or breadboard. They will be juicy and slippery and you do not want them rolling on the kitchen floor! As soon as the sugar syrup is boiling, turn the heat to medium, then place each pear, one at a time, in a large wooden spoon and carefully ease into the boiling syrup. *Easy, easy!* I want you to imagine how boiling syrup hurts if it splatters you. Add a few drops of vanilla extract, cover the pot, and let the pears boil gently for 20 minutes. Take a wooden spoon (if a metal spoon is all you have, use it but be careful as it may cut into the fruit) and gently turn them in the syrup. Replace the cover and continue to cook for 10 more minutes. This timing may not be exact because some pears are smaller than others and some are riper. Test them by gently pricking them with a pointed knife or sharp-pointed little fork before removing from the syrup. If they feel soft, not mushy, they are done.

SECOND:

Place a good-size bowl on the counter or kitchen table. Carefully carry the pot over to the bowl (using pot holders) and, most carefully, spoon the pears into the bowl. Slowly, holding the handle with both hands, pour the syrup over them. Cool to room temperature,* then put them in the refrigerator to chill.

THIRD:

When ready to serve, lift the pears out of the syrup with a slotted spoon, letting *all the liquid drain off* before placing each pear in an individual glass serving bowl or china dish. Cover the pears just before serving with warm Chocolate Sauce (see page 47).

Note: The leftover syrup may be used the next time you make a gelatine dessert. Use 1 cup of this syrup in place of 1 cup of the water in the instructions. The syrup may be kept at least a week in a covered jar in the refrigerator.

WHAT YOU'LL NEED:

measuring cup	little pointed knife or fork
large pot with cover	good-size bowl
stirring spoon	2 pot holders
paring knife	slotted spoon
plate or breadboard	individual glass serving bowls
large wooden spoon	or china dishes

Sauce au Chocolat

CHOCOLATE SAUCE

Serves 4

4 squares bitter cooking chocolate
1 tablespoon butter
1 cup sugar
½ cup light cream or half-and-half
1 tablespoon vanilla extract

FIRST:

Melt* 4 squares of bitter cooking chocolate with 1 tablespoon
butter in the top of a small double boiler. (The water in the lower
half of double boiler should be boiling.*) Cover. Put 1 cup of
sugar and ½ cup of light cream or half-and-half in a small pot.
Stir* over medium heat just until the sugar melts. Remove from
the heat. When the chocolate is melted, add the sugar mixture to
the chocolate.

SECOND:

Remove the top of the double boiler and place directly on a low
fire. Stir constantly until the mixture boils. Boil, without stirring, for 5 to 10 minutes until the sauce begins to thicken. (But
be sure not to have your heat too high because chocolate has a
tendency to burn easily.) Add 1 tablespoon vanilla extract and
stir it in thoroughly. Return the top to the double boiler, turn the
heat low, and leave until ready to use. Serve in a pretty sauce
bowl with a little ladle.

Note: This sauce may be made ahead of time and left in the refrigerator in a covered container. When ready to use, put it in the top of the double boiler with low heat underneath until it melts and is smooth again. When reheating it may be necessary to use a little extra cream or half-and-half.

WHAT YOU'LL NEED:

small double boiler with cover   measuring spoons
measuring cup   sauce bowl
small pot   little ladle
stirring spoon

·4·
KATINAKI
OF GREECE

Kali Imera:

My name is Katinaki and I live in Greece. The town in which I live is very old. It is called Megara and overlooks the sea. Megara is not far from Athens and is on the narrow strip of land that leads to the Peloponnesus with the Gulf of Corinth on one side and the Saronic Gulf on the other.

Where we live, the sea is blue and green and, on a clear day, if I am lucky, I can see an island far away. When our fishing boats go out to sea, their white sails look beautiful against the sky. Do you know that the history books say that the people of Megara have always been more beautiful than any other people here in Greece? Perhaps it's because we love to laugh and dance. I wish you could see the festivals we have in the village square. When we have a festival, we dress up in the old-style clothes and they are so beautiful that many famous artists have painted pictures of our dancers, with the wide embroidered skirts of the women flying in the wind. No matter how far you go away, they say, if you were born in Megara you can be sure you will return. Up to now I've never known whether to believe this, but at last I know it's true because our Uncle Nicholas is coming home today.

You must excuse me, I always talk this fast when I get

excited. Just let me say I live on a little farm, in a small whitewashed house that shines brightly in the sun. We have many olive trees so we have shade when the sun grows hot in summer, and a vineyard in the back that grows many grapes to take to market, *Patēra* and *Mitēra* live in the house as do my brothers, Constantine and Nicholas. Constantine is just thirteen and foolish enough to think himself a man! Our little Nikos is a dreadful tease but gay and very funny. He makes me giggle a lot so I don't mind if he follows me around.

Patēra raises special grapes for the Greek *retsina* wine, some olives for oil, and sometimes chickens. You might say we are poor but, all the same, we laugh a lot and love to listen to our patēra tell us stories about ancient Greece. Constantine prefers to hear how Patēra fought the Nazis in the war and the Communists who tried to take our country after that. That was when Patēra hurt his leg and that's why, he says, he cannot work too hard. We tell him we do not mind if we'll never be richer than we are. But sometimes I've heard Mitēra say, "Isn't there your rich Uncle Nicholas?"

Now Uncle Nicholas is almost here. His ship comes in today. It has traveled a long way — from far-off America! Our Uncle Nicholas is very old. He's not my patēra's brother but my grandfather's brother, and he's been living in America for fifty years. I don't know if it's a little town or city but it's some place called Chicago. Uncle Nicholas had a Greek *taverna* in Chicago so I suppose he's very,

very rich! His wife, our Aunt Maria, has joined the Saints in Heaven. They never had a child so Uncle Nicholas is very lonely. He wrote us that he misses Greece and wants to see Megara before he joins our Aunt Maria and the Saints.

Mitēra doesn't think our house is good enough but Patēra said it is our home, and if Uncle Nicholas wants to be with us he'll have to take us as we are. I know that Mitēra hopes he'll spend a little money to fix things up a bit, but Patēra said, "I'd rather he sent Constantine to school in Athens. But let's not expect that much."

Just now Patēra clapped his hands together and reminded us we have work to do. "Enough of talk!" he said. "We all have things to do without wondering what other people may do for us! Katinaki, go at once and help your mitēra get the food ready that Uncle Nicholas can't wait to taste."

Patēra was talking about the last letter Uncle Nicholas wrote in which he said he was hungry as a bear for the things he used to eat as a young man in Megara. So now I must join Mitēra in the kitchen. I've been helping her cook since I was six or seven. This is one thing I love to do because the kitchen is bright and sunny and, when the food is on the fire, it smells so good I feel warm and hungry. It's peaceful, too. Through the window one sees the sea and Mitēra always sings an ancient Grecian song whenever she gets busy. Does it not seem strange to you that the things our uncle ate so long ago are the same things we eat today? *Soupa Avegolemono, Hunkar Bengendi* (they say it's been a favorite of the kings), with *Rizogalo* and *Yiaourtopeta* for dessert. Imagine! Two desserts to show Uncle Nicholas we're glad to have him come. Later I'll tell you how everything is done.

Herete,
Katinaki

Soupa Avegolemono

CHICKEN SOUP WITH EGG AND LEMON SAUCE

Serves 8

2 quarts homemade chicken broth
    or
4 14-ounce cans clear, unconcentrated chicken soup
½ cup rice (not Instant)
4 eggs
1 tablespoon strained, fresh lemon juice
salt

FIRST:

Use a large pot (with a cover) to bring 2 quarts homemade chicken broth or 4 14-ounce cans clear, unconcentrated chicken soup to a boil.* Add ½ cup rice (not Instant), stir* once with a wooden spoon, cover the pan, and boil for 20 minutes. Remove pot from fire with 2 pot holders and cool for a few minutes before adding to eggs.

SECOND:

Break 4 eggs* into a large mixing bowl. Beat* with an egg beater or a whisk until they turn light in color. Two or three minutes time should do the trick although, of course, it depends on the size of the eggs. An electric mixer helps here but an egg beater will do. Cut a lemon in half and squeeze out 1 tablespoon lemon juice in a juicer or by hand through a fine strainer (no bits — no seeds!). Add to the eggs and continue to beat a little more.

Take a ladle and gradually add the liquid part of the soup to the beaten eggs. Beat without stopping so that the soup and the eggs are thoroughly mixed. Continue to do this until the soup is all added to the bowl. Pour the soup back into the pot.

THIRD:
Turn the heat on (not too high) and gently beat with a wooden spoon until the soup begins to thicken. When it is thick enough, it should look like custard sauce or heavy cream. *But be careful not to let it boil.* If it boils, the soup will be full of scrambled eggs. Just before serving, taste it and add enough salt to satisfy your taste. Warm* the soup dishes slightly and serve.

Note: The sauce made from eggs and lemon juice is a very important part of Greek cooking and is often added to other things like fish or meat stews.

WHAT YOU'LL NEED:

large pot with a cover
measuring cup
wooden spoon
2 pot holders
large mixing bowl
measuring spoons

electric mixer or egg beater
   or whisk
juicer or fine strainer
ladle
soup dishes

Hunkar Begendi

LAMB STEW WITH EGGPLANT PURÉE

Preheat oven* to 400° / Serves 6 to 8

THE LAMB

2 pounds lamb (off leg)
3 onions (4 to 5 inches wide)
¼ pound butter (1 stick)
3 teaspoons tomato paste
1 cup water
1 teaspoon salt
½ teaspoon ground, black
   pepper
finely chopped parsley

THE EGGPLANT PURÉE

2 large eggplants
¼ pound butter (1 stick)
1 cup heavy cream
1 cup milk
½ cup grated Parmesan cheese
   (2 ounces) (may be bought
   in a package)
½ cup bread crumbs (may be
   bought in a package)
½ teaspoon salt
¼ teaspoon ground, black
   pepper

The Lamb

FIRST:

Ask your butcher to cut 2 pounds of lamb off the leg. Put it on a breadboard and cut into pieces, about the size and shape of dominoes. Shove the lamb to one side. Peel* 3 onions, place them on the board, and grate* on a medium grater.

SECOND:

Melt* ¼ pound of butter in your largest frying pan (with a cover). Turn the heat to moderate, put the meat and onions in the pan, and brown in the butter. Turn the meat from side to side with a wooden spoon and watch carefully until it loses all raw color. Put 3 teaspoons of tomato paste in a small bowl, add 1 cup of water, 1 teaspoon salt, and ½ teaspoon ground, black pepper, and mix thoroughly with a small spoon. Pour over the meat, stir*, and bring to a boil.* Cover the pan, reduce the flame, and simmer* for 2 hours until the meat is done. Check after five minutes to make sure it is simmering, not boiling. No need to stir.

The Eggplant Purée

FIRST:

As soon as the meat is covered and left to simmer, prick 2 large eggplants with a pointed paring knife, at least 4 times each. Just pierce the skin lightly. This will allow any steam caught within the eggplants to escape as they cook. Place them *whole* in an oven pan (any pan, deep or shallow, will do). Bake the eggplants in a preheated 400° oven for 1 hour or until they feel tender when you test by pricking with a long-handled fork. Use 2 pot holders to remove the pan from the oven but allow eggplants to cool before trying to handle them. This should take approximately half an hour. Once they are cool enough to touch, take the paring knife and pull off the skins. It will be easy to do this. Put the eggplants in a large mixing bowl and squash them to a pulp with a masher. Melt ¼ pound butter in a small pot and add to eggplants along with 1 cup of cream, 1 cup of milk, ½ cup grated Parmesan cheese, and ½ cup bread crumbs. Season with ½ teaspoon salt and ¼ teaspoon pepper. Transfer from the bowl to a large pot. Place the pot on the stove, turn the heat to moderate, and stir without stopping until the mixture comes to a boil and starts to thicken. It will seem very runny but after it starts to boil, it will thicken until it reminds you of oatmeal.

SECOND:

After it has come to a boil, turn the heat down and allow the eggplant mixture to simmer for 20 minutes, stirring every now and then to be sure it doesn't stick to the bottom of the pot. Otherwise it may burn and the least burn or scorch* will ruin the taste of the whole dish, so be very careful here.

Note: Do not serve the lamb on a flat platter because you will have lots of tomato sauce which might easily run over the sides of the platter. You are going to need a nice, deep serving bowl. The sort that would be right for any stew. After arranging in the bowl, garnish* with finely chopped parsley. The eggplant purée should be served in a good-size vegetable dish. I envy you eating this for the first time! And what compliments you will get!

WHAT YOU'LL NEED:

breadboard	oven pan
kitchen knife	long-handled fork
pointed paring knife	2 pot holders
medium grater	large mixing bowl
large frying pan (with cover)	masher
large wooden spoon	small pot
small bowl	large pot
measuring cup	stirring spoons
measuring spoons	deep serving bowl
small spoon	good-size vegetable dish

Rizogalo

RICE PUDDING WITH CINNAMON

Best prepared the day before / Serves 8

2 cups water
4 cups milk
½ cup rice (not Instant)
4 eggs
1 cup sugar
1 teaspoon salt
2 teaspoons vanilla extract
¼ cup seedless raisins (washed)
powdered cinnamon

FIRST:

Put 2 cups of water and 4 cups of milk in a large pot. Bring to a simmer* then add ½ cup of rice (not Instant), stirring* just once when the rice is first added. Cover the pot and continue to simmer for about ¾ hour or until the mixture is thick and the rice is soft. Remove from stove and let cool a little.

SECOND:

Separate 4 eggs* and store the whites* in a covered jar in the refrigerator (they may be used for meringues). Beat* the egg yolks, gradually adding 1 cup sugar. Continue beating until light in color and very smooth and thick. This is best done by using an electric mixer but may also be accomplished by using a rotary egg beater or whisk. Be sure to use a large bowl, because the cooled rice mixture is going to be added to the eggs. When ready to mix (when the rice is cool and the egg mixture is beaten), put the bowl on the kitchen table or counter and *gradually* add the rice, mixing and stirring with a large spoon. Do not stop until everything is well combined and be sure to scrape the bottom of the bowl as you mix in the rice, being certain that none of the egg remains unmixed. Stir in 1 teaspoon salt and 2 teaspoons of vanilla extract. Stir in ¼ cup of washed seedless raisins.

THIRD:

Use a rubber spatula or large spoon to push everything into the pot and replace on the stove. Cook it over *low* heat for 2 to 3 minutes, *stirring all the time*. Watch that it does not get *too* hot. There is always the dreadful danger of eggs scrambling when they get too hot! Pour all this into a pretty serving dish and sprinkle the top of the pudding generously with powdered cinnamon. Let the bowl stand out in the kitchen until the pudding reaches room temperature,* then put in the refrigerator for at least 5 to 6 hours before serving.

WHAT YOU'LL NEED:

measuring cup
large pot (with cover)
large stirring spoon
electric mixer, egg beater,
   or whisk

large mixing bowl
measuring spoons
rubber spatula or large spoon
pretty serving dish

Yiaourtopeta

YOGURT PIE

Best prepared the day before / Serves 6 to 8

GRAHAM CRACKER CRUST
1⅔ cups loosely packed
  Graham Cracker crumbs
  (1 box)
¼ cup sugar
¼ cup butter (½ stick)
soft butter (about 2
  tablespoons)

THE PIE FILLING
8-ounce package of cream
  cheese (at room
  temperature*)
1 cup plain yogurt
  (½ pint container)
4 tablespoons honey
2 teaspoons vanilla extract

Graham Cracker Crust

FIRST:

If you cannot buy prepackaged Graham Cracker crumbs, place 1 box of graham crackers in a plastic bag and roll them with a rolling pin until they are crumb-size. Mix 1⅔ cups loosely packed Graham Cracker crumbs with ¼ cup sugar in a medium-size bowl. Melt* ¼ cup butter (½ stick) in a small pot over moderate heat. Watch carefully so it does not turn brown because this indicates that the butter is beginning to burn. You could melt the butter in the top of a double boiler with water boiling in the bottom to prevent the butter from burning. Remove from the stove and gradually pour over the Graham Cracker crumbs, moistening the crumbs a little at a time, until they are all well moistened. Mix lightly with a fork until the butter is well distributed.

SECOND:

Put a little soft butter on a folded piece of paper towel and grease* the sides and bottom of an 8-inch oven-proof glass or metal pie plate. Press the crumb mixture evenly into the bottom and sides of the plate. This is easy to do and fun. Use the heel of your hand. The back of a spoon may be used, but I have never found it works half as well as the human hand.

The Pie Filling

FIRST:

Before starting, take your 8-ounce package of cream cheese out of the refrigerator and let it stand until it reaches room temperature. Put the cheese in the small bowl of the electric mixer or cream* by hand with a spoon until soft and smooth. Add 1 cup of plain yogurt and mix *thoroughly*. No lumps, please. Try adding a little of the yogurt at a time to the cream cheese. Stir in 4 tablespoons of honey and 2 teaspoons of vanilla extract.

SECOND:

Pour this into the prepared pie plate, scraping every bit out of the bowl with a rubber spatula or large spoon. Put the pie plate in the refrigerator and refrigerate *at least 24 hours* before serving.

WHAT YOU'LL NEED:

plastic bag	8-inch oven-proof glass or
rolling pin	metal pie plate
measuring cup	small bowl
medium-size bowl	electric mixer or spoon
small pot	measuring spoons
small fork	rubber spatula or large spoon
small piece paper towel	

·5·
ELLA
OF THE NETHERLANDS

Goedendag:

My name is Ella and I live in the city of Leiden in The Netherlands. Leiden is in the southwestern part of our country. Most people call our country Holland. The city of Leiden is a famous place. Did you know that Rembrandt, one of the world's greatest painters, was born here? His paintings are in many museums, and we are proud of him. Leiden is known to Dutch school children as the place where we fought the Spanish invaders years and years ago. It's really not so remarkable because the Dutch people will always fight when invaders come! I wish you could imagine how we fought the Nazis at the start of World War II! Oh, I know a lot about that because *Moeder* has often told me how bravely *Vader* fought and had to hide in attics and in cellars with the fighters of the Underground so Hitler's soldiers couldn't find him. Leiden is also famous for the Pilgrims who fled England centuries ago to practice free religion. They waited here for years. Then they returned to England and boarded a ship called the Mayflower which took them to America. But now Leiden is most famous for its university. My vader is a professor there. He teaches English and English literature, and young people from all over Holland listen to his lectures. I speak a little English and Vader says that's good because few people outside Holland speak our language well.

Last evening, when Vader returned from work, he told Moeder and me that a friend of his, a professor from America, was coming to the university to teach electronics, whatever that may be. Anyway, the professor from America is named Professor Thomas Stephen Martin. They call him an "exchange professor" but I'm not sure I know what that is. The thing that interests *me* is that he has a daughter who is twelve. Just like me. Her name is Sally Sue. That's a name I've never heard before, have you? Well, Vader has invited Professor Thomas Stephen Martin, Mrs. Thomas Stephen Martin, and Sally Sue to have dinner at our house tomorrow night. Sally Sue and her moeder have no friends at all in Holland and Vader says that Moeder and I must make them *our* friends so they feel at home. So, Moeder and I have decided to cook them a fine dinner so they will know at once how many good things we eat in Holland. I am very glad because I love to cook in our pretty kitchen with our Delft tiles on the walls. Delft tiles are white with blue pictures on them of cows and windmills.

I keep thinking of the many things I shall tell Sally Sue. She has so much to learn! About the Holland dikes which are thick enough to hold back the sea, and wide enough to have roads on top. Did you know that's the meaning of the word *Netherlands*? The dikes had to be built higher than the sea. After they had built the dikes, they cleared the land of salt and sea water, and we grow things no other country can grow as well. Like miles and miles of tulips and hyacinths and daffodils. If you could see how beautiful they are in spring! I'm afraid I can't describe them! All I can say is, Sally Sue will just have to wait and see. And the cows! There are cows all over Holland. They give *so* much milk, we eat cheese at almost every meal. But there's still too much, so we have to export a lot, sometimes as far as America.

I must tell Sally Sue about the wooden shoes which we call *Klompen*. I often wonder why they are called that. Maybe it is because when we walk in them they make a funny sound like, "klomp, klomp, klomp." And about the country dogs, big and strong enough to pull wooden carts to market filled with vegetables, cheese, and cans of milk. Of course, one doesn't see them every place since Holland is very modern now, but I'm sure Vader will take Sally Sue and me to Volendam and Marken where the townspeople still wear peasant dress with klompen on their feet! If Sally Sue has seen Dutch dolls, she must know exactly how they look.

Now Moeder is in the kitchen. I can hear her calling me. I shall be very busy. If I try very hard, Vader will be proud of me. I must remember to tell myself, "Ella, take your time." I'm afraid when I am excited, I hurry much too much. I know things turn out better if you never rush. I promise to be careful and not to spoil a thing. I want Professor Thomas Stephen Martin and his family to love our good Dutch cooking. Especially the things we're going to cook for them: *Eieren Gevuld met Kaas; Var-*

kenscrib, *Aardappelpuree*, and *Room Pudding* with a lovely *saus*. I can make these things all by myself. What do you think Sally Sue will think of me?

Tot weerziens,
Ella

Eieren Gevuld met Kaas

EGGS STUFFED WITH CHEESE

Serves 6

6 eggs
2 tablespoons *finely* grated Edam cheese
¼ cup butter (½ stick)
¼ teaspoon salt
¼ teaspoon ground, black pepper
mayonnaise (optional)
6 fresh lettuce leaves
3 teaspoons finely chopped fresh parsley

FIRST:

Boil* 6 eggs until hard (see Page 16). When cool enough to handle, peel* them, and carefully cut them into halves lengthwise. Take a small fork and gently push the yolks out into a sieve. Set the sieve over a small mixing bowl and rub the yolks into the bowl with a small spoon. Scrape the underside of the sieve so you do not waste a bit. Using the *finest* side of a grater,* grate 2 tablespoons of Edam into the bowl, and mix thoroughly with the small fork.

SECOND:

Melt* ¼ cup butter (½ stick) in a small pot. Add to the egg and cheese. Mix thoroughly, then season with ¼ teaspoon of salt and ¼ teaspoon of ground, black pepper. If you want the mixture to be creamier, add a little mayonnaise.

THIRD:

Use a very small spoon to fill the pockets of the emptied egg halves with this mixture. Place all the halves on a plate, cover with waxed paper, and chill for at least one hour in the refrigerator. When ready to serve, put 6 fresh lettuce leaves (rinsed in cold water and dried with paper towels) on 6 individual plates, set 2 filled egg halves on each lettuce leaf, sprinkle with finely chopped fresh parsley, and serve very cold.

WHAT YOU'LL NEED:

pot	small pot
knife	measuring spoons
small fork	very small spoon
sieve	plate
small spoon	waxed paper
small mixing bowl	paper towels
fine grater	6 plates

Varkenscrib

ROLLED RIB OF PORK WITH APPLES

Preheat oven* to 325° / Serves 8

4-pound rolled rib (loin) of pork
¼ pound butter (1 stick)
1 teaspoon salt
½ teaspoon ground, black pepper
1 teaspoon dried marjoram
warm water (approximately 1½ cups)
2 large eating apples

FIRST:

Have your butcher prepare a 4-pound rolled rib of pork. This is lean meat and goes a long way. It is good eaten either hot or cold. Put ¼ pound of butter in a shallow baking pan, approximately 2 inches deep and large enough to fit pork roll, turn the oven heat to 325° and, when the oven is ready, put the pan in the oven on the center rack. When the butter has melted,* take 2 pot holders and remove the pan to the counter or the kitchen table — leave the oven on at 325°. Put the rolled pork in the pan, sprinkle it all over with 1 teaspoon of salt, ½ teaspoon of pepper, and 1 teaspoon of dried marjoram. Return the pan to the oven and use the pot holders as the pan is still apt to be hot.

SECOND:

Roast the pork for half an hour without opening the oven door. Heat a little water in a small pot, then start to baste* by spooning the water with a large kitchen spoon over the roast. One large kitchen-spoonful at a time will just do. Close the oven door, then be sure to remember to baste every 15 minutes, until there is enough liquid in the bottom of the pan so no more need be added. Be sure not to add too much water or the gravy will be thin. After the first hour, take a paring knife and peel,* core,* and slice 2 large eating apples into ½-inch slices. With one pot holder in each hand, carefully pull the pan halfway out. With a long-handled kitchen spoon, place the apple slices around the roast, then push the pan back into the oven and roast the pork another hour. Continue to baste, as before, every 15 minutes — this time without adding water — using the juices in the pan to moisten the apples as well as the meat.

THIRD:

When the second hour is up, take the pot holders and carefully remove the pan to the counter or the kitchen table. With a pair of kitchen scissors, cut the strings the butcher put around the roast. Pull them off, one by one, and throw them away. Place the roast on a serving platter, spoon the apples around it, and keep it warm while you prepare the gravy.

To keep the roast warm:
Turn the oven off, put the serving platter in the oven and leave the oven door open. If you closed the oven door, the meat would continue to cook and you do not want to dry it out.

To prepare the gravy:
You will notice that the fat has risen to the top of the liquid in the pan. Have a small bowl beside you and gently spoon out as much fat as possible, trying not to disturb the brown gravy at the bottom of the pan. Warm* the gravy boat or bowl and pour the gravy into it. Serve the roast with mashed potatoes and any vegetable you prefer, although brussel sprouts are often used in Holland.

WHAT YOU'LL NEED:

shallow baking pan	long-handled kitchen spoon
2 pot holders	kitchen scissors
measuring spoons	serving platter
small pot	small bowl
large kitchen spoon	small spoon
paring knife	gravy boat or bowl
slicing knife	

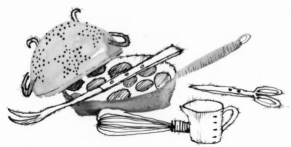

Aardappelpuree

MASHED POTATOES

Serves 6

½ teaspoon salt
4 large potatoes (approximately 6 inches long)
3 tablespoons butter
½ cup milk
½ teaspoon salt
¼ teaspoon ground, black pepper
pinch nutmeg (optional)
extra butter (optional)
1 teaspoon finely chopped fresh parsley

FIRST:

Fill a good-size pot ⅔ full of water. Stir* in ½ teaspoon salt. Put the pot over high heat and let the water come to a strong boil.* Use a potato peeler or paring knife to peel* 4 large potatoes. When peeled, cut the potatoes into halves, then slide them gently into the boiling water with a long-handled spoon. Be careful not to let them splash into the pot. Continue to boil at high heat until the potatoes feel tender when tested with a pointed knife or fork. (Fork can go easily into center of potatoes.) The *exact* timing is difficult to give, as it depends on the size of the potatoes. The average time is about 20 minutes. When the potatoes are tender, turn off the heat, carefully carry the pot (using 2 pot holders) to the sink and, with a slotted spoon, remove the potatoes to a colander and let them drain. Pour the water out of the pot into the sink. You are going to need the pot again.

SECOND:

Place a potato ricer over the empty pot. Take the potatoes up in a spoon, one or two at a time, put them in the ricer and mash them into the pot. If you do not have a potato ricer, use a masher but be sure not to leave any lumps. This must be done while the potatoes are still hot. Continue until all are mashed. Put 2 table-spoons of butter into the riced potatoes. Warm ½ cup of milk in a small pot (do not boil) and add to the potatoes. Beat with a large wooden spoon. Continue to beat until the potato mixture is very smooth and creamy. No lumps, please! Season with ½ teaspoon of salt and ¼ teaspoon of pepper. If you enjoy the taste of nutmeg, you may add a little pinch.

THIRD:

Warm* a vegetable dish. Put in the mashed potatoes and sprinkle the top with 1 teaspoon finely chopped parsley. If you want to be extra fancy, you may stick a piece of butter on top of the pota-toes before sprinkling on the parsley.

Note: If for any reason the mashed potatoes must wait, put them in the top of a large double boiler over medium heat, with water in lower half just simmering, but not for long or they may dry out. If they do get dry, add a little milk and stir vigorously before you serve.

WHAT YOU'LL NEED:

good-size pot	colander
measuring spoons	potato ricer or masher
potato peeler or paring knife	measuring cup
slicing knife	small pot
long-handled spoon	large wooden spoon
small pointed knife or fork	vegetable dish
2 pot holders	large double boiler (optional)
slotted spoon	

Room Pudding

CREAM PUDDING

Best prepared the day before / Serves 8

2 tablespoons plain gelatin (2 envelopes)
½ cup water (cold)
½ cup milk
2 cups heavy cream
½ cup sugar
1 cup heavy cream (for whipping)
1 tablespoon vanilla extract
12 sugar-cream-filled wafers
Raspberry Sauce (see page 21)

FIRST:

Use a teaspoon to stir* 2 tablespoons of gelatin into ½ cup of cold water in a small bowl. Let it stand until it thickens (about 5 minutes). Meanwhile put ½ cup of milk and 2 cups of heavy cream and ½ cup sugar into a medium-size pot, turn the heat to medium, and bring to a boil.* Watch carefully as milk has a tendency to boil all of a sudden and rise out of the pot — and that makes an awful mess! When the milk mixture is boiling, add the gelatin, scraping every bit into the pot with a rubber spatula or spoon. Stir until it is dissolved. *This is important.* Remove the pot from the stove (using a potholder) and immediately pour the contents of the pot into a bowl and leave it until it cools to room temperature.* This should take about an hour. So, now you have a little time to do other things. You could prepare

the Raspberry Sauce but don't leave the pudding *too long* as it's
going to thicken as it cools, at which time you will have to be on
hand.

SECOND:

When the mixture starts to thicken, whip 1 cup of whipping
cream with an electric mixer or an egg beater until it is very
thick. With rubber spatula or spoon, fold* it into the bowl of
pudding until everything is mixed. Stir in 1 tablespoon of vanilla
extract. Break 12 sugar-cream-filled wafers into thirds and
drop the little pieces into the bowl. Stir carefully so as not to
break them. Just cover gently with the pudding mixture. Put a
ring mold, or any other mold you prefer under the cold water
tap so the mold is moist, but be sure to pour out any extra water.
Now, pour the pudding into the mold, scraping the bowl with
the rubber spatula or spoon so as not to waste a bit. Cover the
filled mold with wax paper so the pudding will not pick up any
refrigerator odors, place the mold in the refrigerator, and leave
it for at least 4 hours until firmly set. When ready to serve, unmold (See note) on a cold serving platter and serve with Raspberry Sauce in a sauce boat or bowl.

Note: The best way to unmold is to partly fill the kitchen sink
with hot (not scalding) water. Take the ring mold and *quickly*
dip it up and down and in and out of the water (be careful not
to let the water run over into the mold!). Do this several times.
Put the mold on the counter or kitchen table, and run a thin
knife around all the inside edges of the mold without cutting
into the pudding. Place the serving plate on top of the mold and
with your thumbs on the bottom edges of the plate and the rest
of your fingers underneath the mold, invert it quickly. In other
words, turn the whole thing upside down. Tap the top of the
mold, as it stands on the plate, with a heavy knife handle. Tap it
here and tap it there. The pudding should fall out. Gently lift off

the mold. But if it doesn't fall out of the mold at once, put a kitchen cloth in very hot water, quickly wring it out and lay it over the top of the mold. This should do the trick!

WHAT YOU'LL NEED:

teaspoon
small bowl
measuring spoons
measuring cup
medium-size pot
rubber spatula or spoon
2 potholders
bowl
electric mixer or egg beater
ring mold

wax paper
electric blendor (if you have
  one)
good-size sieve
bowl
spoon
thin knife
serving plate
sauce boat or bowl
heavy knife

·6·
ROSALINA
OF ITALY

Buon giorno:

I am Rosalina and my *papá* owns a restaurant. We are a big family and we live in Venice, Italy. In all the world there is no place as beautiful as Venice. All the houses, the churches, the markets, the shops and *piazze* (I think you call them public squares) are built along canals. When it is too far to walk, you ride in *gondole* which are thin black boats with *gondolieri* who stand at the back and push a long stick, like an oar, through the water of the canal. Venice has motor boats instead of buses as they have in other cities. But I do not care for them. I love the old-fashioned gondole like the one Papá takes to market to bring back the fresh vegetables, the fish, the veal, the lamb, and the sweet butter and olive oil from Lucca he uses in his restaurant.

Our restaurant is called *"Mio Amore"* (which means "my love"), and the rooms we live in are on the second floor. We are to be found three bridgs to the left, then two bridges to the right of the Grand Canal — not too far from the Rialto (the bridge over the Grand Canal). If we two could walk together, I could show you easily. Trying to describe the way is difficult. It is not always easy to find your way in Venice through the narrow streets that go winding here and there.

Bene, I was saying, Papá has the kind of restaurant which in Italy we call a *trattoria.* It is not an elegant place where foreign tourists come, but a small place which all Venetians know serves the best food of our region. Papá is the *best* chef in Italy. Of course, I've never been to other restaurants, but I know this to be true because Papá told me so and he knows everything. Not only about cooking but about Italian opera, too.

It is marvelous to hear him sing while he is working in the kitchen. When he chops, he sings the fastest arias, but when he's watching his sauces simmer, he sings as if afraid to awaken someone. *Fantastico! Mamma* said that when I was very small, I never gave her trouble. All she had to do was put me in the kitchen to watch Papá cook and listen to his songs. Even now, I prefer doing this to any-thing, but I must help Mamma because she's always busy. When she is not working with Papá in the kitchen, she puts on her white apron and serves the customers out front.

She works very hard and still has time to take care of the children. I have eight brothers and sisters. I am the eldest so I have to help Mamma with the little ones. Some-one has to watch that the *bambini* do not fall in the canal.

Angelina came to visit today. She is Mamma's niece, She lives in the mountains near Asolo and whenever there is a new baby on the way, Angelina comes! When she ar-rived she asked Papá if he wished her to help him in the kitchen. She likes the kitchen best. I know why. Because she likes to eat so much! *Quella é grossa!* That one is fat!

Papá just smiled like he was Tonio, our cat, who had swallowed a mouse. Then he made me proud. "Dear Angelina, go upstairs," he said. "Help Maria with the children. Rosalina is a big girl now. *She* will help me in the kitchen." Oh, Papá, how I love you!

I have been so busy, I had to stop writing. But to continue. Now several days have gone since Angelina came. Mamma still waits upstairs for the baby but Papá and I are busy in the kitchen morning, noon, and night.

I am learning fast. Already I can make the *Stracciatella* for which Papá's name is famous. And I can make *Risotto alla Marinara*, a marvelous Venetian rice with shrimp and Parmesan, but *no* tomato sauce. Papá says they may have their tomato sauce in Sicily and Naples! Everyone who comes to the trattoria loves Papá's *Cioccolato alla Crema*. It's their favorite dessert.

Yesterday, a lady said, "Little one, tell your papá this is the best chocolate dessert in Italy." I said *"Si, Signora, grazie."* I did not tell her I'd made it by myself! But I was very proud.

Arrivederci,
Rosalina

Stracciatella

CHICKEN BROTH WITH BEATEN EGG

Serves 6

1½ quarts clear chicken broth
     or
3½-4 14-ounce cans unconcentrated chicken broth
3 eggs
3 tablespoons freshly grated Parmesan cheese
2 tablespoons farina
¼ teaspoon salt
¼ cup freshly chopped parsley
extra Parmesan cheese (optional)

FIRST:

Measure out 1½ quarts clear chicken broth in a good-size pot, but wait before putting it on the stove. Break 3 eggs* into a small bowl. Beat* the eggs with a wire whisk or egg beater until completely blended. Add 3 tablespoons freshly grated Parmesan cheese into the bowl and add 2 tablespoons of farina, and ¼ teaspoon salt. Beat well. Finally, add ½ cup of the broth you have measured out. Stir* well.

SECOND:

Put the pot on the stove. Turn the heat to high and bring the rest of the broth to a boil.* Add the contents of the bowl to the boiling soup. There are several ways of doing this, but whichever way you do it, do it gradually . . . a little at a time. Either dribble the egg mixture into the boiling soup by holding the bowl in your left hand while you beat the broth madly with a wire whisk or spoon in your right hand, or spoon it into the soup, a little at a time. Whichever way is easiest for *you*. But whatever you do, do not forget to beat while adding the egg mixture and for several minutes after it has been added. The mixture will look fluffy.

THIRD:

Warm* the soup bowls or plates. Bring the broth back to a boil for 1 minute, remove the pot from the stove, and stir in ¼ cup of freshly chopped parsley. Spoon even amounts into heated soup bowls or soup plates and serve immediately. You may serve extra freshly grated Parmesan cheese in a side bowl, if you like. Many people enjoy a sprinkling of extra Parmesan cheese on their broth.

WHAT YOU'LL NEED:

quart measure or measuring
   cup
good-size pot
small bowl
wire whisk or egg beater

grater
measuring spoons
stirring spoon
soup bowls or plates
small serving bowl

Risotto alla Marinara
RICE WITH SEAFOOD
Serves 4 to 6

1½ cups water
1 cup clear chicken broth
   (approximately 1 can unconcentrated broth)
1 teaspoon salt
1 teaspoon butter

1 cup white rice (not Instant)
¼ pound butter (1 stick)
½ cup freshly grated Parmesan cheese
1 pound medium-size cooked shrimp
   (shelled, de-veined, and thawed if frozen)
1 teaspoon freshly chopped parsley
additional freshly grated Parmesan cheese

FIRST:

Put 1½ cups water and 1 cup clear chicken broth in a good-size pot, turn the heat on high, and bring mixture to a boil.* Stir* in 1 teaspoon salt and 1 teaspoon of butter. Gradually add 1 cup of rice, a little at a time, so the water does not stop boiling. This is important. When all the rice is added, stir just once (preferably with a fork) then cover the pot, turn the heat on *low*, and continue to cook for 25 to 30 minutes or until the rice is tender, but not mushy, and all the water is absorbed.

SECOND:

Melt* ¼ pound butter in a small pot. Stir the melted butter into the rice. Grate* ½ cup Parmesan cheese. Add to rice with 1 pound medium-size cooked shrimp. Warm* the serving platter fill it with the rice and shrimp, decorate* the top with 1 teaspoon of freshly chopped parsley, and serve it hot. Warm plates, please, and a side bowl of freshly grated Parmesan cheese to sprinkle on the individual portions.

WHAT YOU'LL NEED:

measuring cup	small pot
good-size pot with cover	grater
measuring spoons	serving platter
stirring spoon	serving bowl
fork	

Cioccolato alla Crema

CHOCOLATE CREAM

Best prepared the day before / Serves 8

1 tablespoon plain gelatin
  (1 envelope)
¼ cup cold water
½ cup boiling water
4 squares bitter cooking
  chocolate
1 cup half-and-half or light
  cream
5 eggs
1 cup sugar
1 tablespoon vanilla extract

GARNISH
1 cup heavy cream
  (for whipping)
¼ cup confectioner's sugar
1 tablespoon vanilla extract
chocolate sprinkles

FIRST:

Take a measuring cup and stir* 1 tablespoon gelatin in ¼ cup cold water until the gelatin is moistened. Let stand for 5 minutes. While waiting, boil* ½ cup water in a small pot. Pour the boiling water into the cup and stir until the gelatin is dissolved.

SECOND:

Put 4 squares of bitter cooking chocolate in the top of a double boiler, with water already boiling in the bottom half. Add 1 cup of half-and-half or light cream. Turn the heat to medium and allow the chocolate to dissolve. Stir occasionally to mix it with the cream. Remove the top of the double boiler from the heat and scrape the contents into a large mixing bowl with a wooden spoon or rubber spatula. Allow it to cool for a minute or two.

THIRD:

Separate 5 eggs* (the yolks in a small bowl, the whites in a larger bowl) and beat* the yolks with 1 cup of sugar, preferably with an electric mixer but, in any case, beat it until the mixture is smooth and creamy. Add to the chocolate mixture and stir thoroughly. Add the dissolved gelatin and 1 tablespoon of vanilla extract. Mix everything very, very well.

FOURTH:

Wash the beaters you used for the egg yolks until no egg yolk remains. Then beat 5 egg whites until firm so when you pull the beaters out of the mixture, it stands up in little peaks like "donkey ears." Gently fold* into chocolate mixture. Use a rubber spatula or wooden spoon. Be sure to work down to the bottom of the bowl since some of the chocolate may be stuck down there. It is important to mix everything together. This delicious dessert may be served in several ways — either in a large serving bowl or in individual custard cups or pretty serving bowls. Refrigerate at least 6 hours. When ready to serve, decorate* the top or tops with the following garnish: Mix 1 cup of heavy cream, ¼ cup of confectioner's sugar, and 1 tablespoon vanilla extract. Beat until stiff. Spread with a spatula on chocolate cream and decorate* with a thick covering of chocolate sprinkles. These sprinkles are used a great deal in Italy for all chocolate desserts. They make a very pretty finish.

WHAT YOU'LL NEED:

measuring cup	rubber spatula or wooden
stirring spoon	spoon
measuring spoons	electric mixer or egg beater
small pot	large serving bowl or
double boiler	individual custard cups
3 bowls (1 small, 2 large)	or serving bowls

·7·
SHOKO
OF JAPAN

Ohayo gozaimasu:

My name is Shoko. I am a Japanese girl and I live in the largest city in the world, Tokyo. I live with my honorable *Papa-san* and *Mama-san* and my little brother, whom we call Ito Chan. Today is a most happy day because tomorrow is an important holiday. Tomorrow is *Hina Matsuri* or the Girls' Festival of the Dolls. Each year, on March the third, we have this holiday. All the girls in Japan wait with patient joy for the Festival of the Dolls to come.

Many Japanese families have collections of beautiful dolls. Some of the collections of dolls are so old and venerable that they have belonged to families for many generations. On the day of the Festival, the beautiful dolls are taken from their place of storage where they have been sleeping for a whole long year, unwrapped most carefully, and placed on shelves to be admired for a week. Today I will not think that a week has only seven days, because it makes me sad to remember that at the end of the seventh day, the dolls will be wrapped up again and returned to the *kura,* which is a storage room that is built of cement, out in the garden.

This morning, I helped Mama-san place our dolls upon the shelves. They are such a great treasure and very, very lovely. And they are like my friends. I know each one so well. I greet each one with a smile, especially the dolls that were my great-great-grandmother's, for they are the oldest dolls and are dressed like the Emperor and Empress in embroidered *kimono* of pure silk. The youngest dolls are those which Papa-san has bought for me. Ten in all, one for each year of my life. He buys them in the stores in the *Ginza*, the big shopping center which each year has new and prettier dolls. There has been a new one bought for me this year but I have not seen it yet. I shall see it tomorrow, when the sun rises on the Festival of the Dolls.

Tomorrow my friends will visit me. Together we shall sit on the cushions on the floor and admire the dolls. Then we shall dine, sitting on the floor as we always do, in front of the lacquered tables with low legs. I am very happy about the Festival of Dolls, but I feel even greater happiness because early tomorrow, before my friends arrive, I shall be permitted to help Mama-san in the kitchen. I have been told by my honorable parent that I may help her prepare the dishes for my friends. It is time, she says, I learned to cook. Then, when I am old enough to marry, I shall know how to please my husband with dishes a Japanese gentleman likes best. It is important for a girl, even as young as I, to learn how to please a husband, and learning to cook is a beginning. Mama-san also says it is necessary to serve all the dishes so the eye is pleased. I will learn how to use pretty porcelain bowls and Mama-san says they must never be too full, for the people of Japan do not "live to eat" but "eat to live."

Our most important food is *Gohan* (which is boiled

rice), so when I have prepared Gohan properly, I shall have learned a great deal, indeed. Also, I shall learn how to make *Chawan-mushi* which is a most delicious dish with steamed custard on the top and clear broth with chicken meat and shrimp and water chestnuts underneath. I shall help prepare *Oyako-domburi* to eat with the rice. Oyako-domburi is chicken cooked with green peas, green onions, and mushrooms. In Japan, we do not eat many sweets but, because this is a holiday, I shall learn to make *Ichigo to Awayuki* to please my friends. This sweet is made with strawberries and the beaten white of egg. While I am in the kitchen, I shall wear my old kimono, but tomorrow I shall put on my best new kimono made of silk. It's a lovely fabric, colored a pastel rose. I shall, of course, wear my *obi,* too. An obi is a sash or girdle that goes around the middle. It is tied so it looks like a big butterfly across my back. Won't you please prepare these dishes from Japan? We like them very much here in Tokyo. I think you will like them, too.

Sayonara,
Shoko

Chawan-mushi

STEAMED BROTH WITH CHICKEN, EGG, AND VEGETABLES

Preheat oven* to 450° / Serves 4

4 cups clear chicken broth
   (approximately 2½ 14-ounce cans)
3 eggs
½ teaspoon salt
2 teaspoons soy sauce
1 teaspoon sugar
1 cup cooked white chicken meat
   (approximately 2 5-ounce jars)
½ cup tiniest cooked shrimp
   (4½-ounce can, or fresh if possible)
1 4-ounce can water chestnuts

FIRST:

Before starting, turn the oven to 450°. Be sure it is ready and hot enough before putting the Chawan-mushi in. Pour 4 cups of clear chicken broth into a good-size pot and warm it slightly. It must not be too hot as eggs are to be added and, if the liquid is too hot, you will have scrambled eggs! Complete disaster! Break 3 eggs* into a small bowl and beat* until they are well mixed. Gradually add a little of the chicken broth, beating without stopping. Take the pot off the fire and slowly pour the eggs into the pot, stirring* constantly and thoroughly. Season the broth with ½ teaspoon of salt, 2 teaspoons of soy sauce, and 1 teaspoon sugar. Stir to mix. Do not return to fire.

SECOND:

Cut 1 cup of cooked white meat of chicken into delicate slivers with a small cutting knife. Put them on a plate. Put ½ cup of the tiniest shrimp on another plate and then open a 4-ounce can of water chestnuts and put them on a third plate. All these things are to be added to the broth in individual oven-proof bowls with lids. Put an even amount of chicken meat, tiny shrimp, and chestnut slices in each bowl. Use a small spoon. Stir the broth once more to be sure it is well mixed with the egg, then ladle it carefully into the bowls, but do not fill the bowls too full. Approximately 1 cup of broth for each person. Leave about ¼ inch at the top. Put the lids on and put the bowls into a large, deep oven pan. When the bowls are in, carry the oven pan to the sink and pour enough hot water from the tap into the pan around the bowls so the water comes halfway up the sides of the bowls. Carry the pan carefully to the preheated oven. Place on center rack, and close oven door.

THIRD:

Leave pan in the oven at 450° for 15 minutes. Then turn the oven down to 350° and continue to cook for another 20 minutes. Take a pot holder in your hand, lift off one of the covers and take a peek to be sure there is a firm layer of custard on top before removing the pan from the oven. It may take a little longer. When the custard is set, take 2 pot holders and carefully remove the pan from the oven. Be very, very careful. Get a firm grip on the pan, very slowly pull it from the oven, and place it carefully on the counter or the kitchen table. Ladle some of the hot water that is around the covered bowls into an empty pot before trying to remove the bowls with pot holders. Even pot holders can burn your fingers if they soak up boiling water! So, please be careful and try not to hurry things. Place each covered bowl on a plate on which you have put a paper or cloth doily or coaster to keep the bowl from sliding. None of these precautions are a lot of trouble, but they are mentioned so you will not hurt yourself. When the lids are lifted, the eggs will have risen to the top and there should be a solid layer of custard on top of every bowl, with the clear broth underneath, filled with so many delicious things (the chicken meat, the tiny shrimps, and the crunchy water chestnuts). This makes for a great surprise and an exciting dish!

WHAT YOU'LL NEED:

measuring cup	3 small plates
good-size pot	4 oven-proof bowls (with lids)
small bowl	small spoon
whisk or stirring spoon	large, deep oven pan
ladle	2 heavy pot holders
measuring spoons	plates
small cutting knife	doilies or coasters

Gohan

JAPANESE-STYLE BOILED RICE

Serves 4

1 cup rice (not Instant)
1 cup plus 3 tablespoons cold water

FIRST:

Put 1 cup of rice in a strainer. Run cold water through the rice, and stir the rice with the fingers of your hand under the running water until the water runs clear. Put the rice in a heavy pot that has a well-fitting lid. Cover it with the cold water and let it stand at least for half an hour.

SECOND:

Cover the pot, turn the heat on high, and quickly bring the water to a rolling boil.* Turn the heat down. Do not lift the cover as steam should stay inside pot. Allow the rice to simmer* for 20 minutes. *Do not stir.* When the 20 minutes are over, turn the heat up while you count slowly to 30, then turn off the heat (if it is an electric stove take the pot off the stove), and let the rice steam within the pot for 10 more minutes before taking off the cover. Warm* a serving dish and spoon rice into it. Serve immediately.

WHAT YOU'LL NEED:

good-size strainer   large spoon
measuring cup   serving dish
heavy pot (with well-fitting lid)

Oyako-domburi

RICE WITH CHICKEN AND VEGETABLES

Serves 4

1 double chicken breast (raw)
  (approximate weight ¾ pound)
2 tablespoons soy sauce
1 overflowing cup raw rice (not Instant)
½ cup clear, unconcentrated chicken broth
pinch of salt
¼ teaspoon sugar
1 4-ounce can sliced mushrooms
1 cup cooked green peas (fresh or frozen, see note)
½ cup sliced green onions (scallions)
¼ teaspoon Monosodium Glutamate
3 eggs

FIRST:

Put 1 double breast of chicken (uncooked) on a breadboard.
Take a paring knife and carefully remove all skin and discard.
Very carefully, remove every bit of bone and gristle and discard. I say carefully because you must try not to waste any of
the chicken meat. Cut the meat into little pieces about the size of
a thimble or a marble. Put them in a small bowl and pour 2
tablespoons of soy sauce over them. Start to prepare the rice (see
page 99) using about 2 extra tablespoons of water. Soak the
chicken pieces in the soy sauce for 30 minutes, turning them
occasionally.

SECOND:

Heat ½ cup of clear chicken broth in a small pot until it simmers.* Remove from fire and season with a pinch of salt and ¼ teaspoon of sugar. Put the chicken and the soy sauce in a 9 or 10-inch frying pan over medium heat. Stir* the chicken pieces in the pan until they lose their raw color. (Do not have the heat too high.) Pour the chicken broth into the pan. Add 1 4-ounce can of sliced mushrooms (without the liquid), 1 cup of cooked peas, and ½ cup of green onions (scallions) sliced across into ¼-inch pieces. Sprinkle in ¼ teaspoon Monosodium Glutamate. Shake the pan and cook uncovered over medium heat for 5 minutes.

THIRD:

While the chicken is cooking, break 3 eggs* in a small bowl and beat* until thoroughly mixed. Pour the eggs into the pan containing the chicken and vegetables. Turn down the heat and shake the pan by the handle to distribute everything, and cook gently for 3 minutes or until the eggs are set and there is just enough sauce to moisten. Warm* a serving bowl, put 4 cups of cooked, hot rice into it, and pour the contents of the frying pan on top. In Japan, this is served in pretty little individual bowls, partly filled with rice and with chicken and vegetables on top. It may be served in the large bowl and dished out onto plates if you have no little bowls.

Note: To shell fresh peas, press the two ends of the pod between your thumbs and forefingers and slide the peas out of the opened pod, into a bowl, with the thumb of your right hand. Throw the pod away. When cooking fresh peas, put them in a pot, just cover with boiling* water, season with salt and pepper, and add 1 teaspoon of butter. Boil furiously (uncovered) for about 15 minutes. When using frozen peas, follow the instructions on the box.

WHAT YOU'LL NEED:

breadboard	small pot
paring knife	stirring spoon
2 small bowls	9 or 10-inch frying pan
measuring spoons	slicing knife
measuring cup	egg beater or whisk
good-size strainer	large serving bowl or
heavy pot (with well-fitting	4 individual bowls
lid)	

Ichigo to Awayuki

STRAWBERRIES WITH MERINGUE

Serves 6

1 box frozen strawberries (thawed)
¼ cup cold water
1 tablespoon plain gelatin (1 envelope)
1 egg (use white only)
plain sugar cookies

FIRST:

Prepare strawberry sauce (see note page 21).

SECOND:

Pour the strawberry sauce into a good-size mixing bowl. Put ¼ cup of cold water into a measuring cup. Sprinkle in 1 table-spoon of plain gelatin and stir* with a teaspoon until the gelatin is mixed thoroughly with the water. Allow the cup to stand for 5 minutes. While waiting, fill a small frying pan half full of water, place it on the heat until the water starts to simmer.* When ready, set the measuring cup in the pan, keeping the pan over low heat. When the gelatin has melted, take it out, and pour it into the strawberry sauce, being sure that every bit is added. (Scrape the cup with a rubber spatula.) Stir well until thoroughly combined.

THIRD:

Separate* 1 egg. Beat* the egg white in an electric mixer or with an egg beater until stiff enough to stand in little peaks like "donkey ears" when the beaters are lifted from the mixture. Add the beaten egg white to the strawberries and, with rubber spatula or wooden spoon, gently fold* in the whites until completely combined. When doing this, do not forget to get down to the bottom of the bowl so not a speck of strawberry sauce is left unmixed. When this is done, you should have a beautiful pink fluff. Spoon it into 6 individual custard cups or little Japanese bowls and place them in the refrigerator (for two or three hours) until set. Eat this with little spoons and a side dish of plain sugar cookies.

WHAT YOU'LL NEED:

electric blendor or good-size
   strainer
wooden spoon
good-size mixing bowl
measuring cup
measuring spoons
teaspoon

small frying pan
rubber spatula
stirring spoon
electric mixer or egg beater
6 custard cups or Japanese
   bowls

·8·
MARÍA TERESA OF SPAIN

Buenos Dias:

My name is María Teresa and I live in Spain on a large *rancho* with *Papá*, *Mamá*, my sisters Catalina, Lucrecia, and Marcelita, and my brothers Juan, Fernando, Roberto, and Tomás. Although we were born on the rancho, it does not belong to us. It belongs to *Señor* Felipe de Gonzáles who is very, very rich and lives in a big house in the city of Seville. I have never seen Seville but perhaps I shall go someday when Papá visits Señor de Gonzáles to talk about the bulls. Papá is the overseer of the rancho and he raises the best bulls in Spain.

I am only ten, but today I feel grownup. Today I shall help Mamá prepare a great *fiesta* for tomorrow. Señor de Gonzáles has planned the feast to honor my oldest brother, Juan. Juan has suddenly become a most important bullfighter. That is a great honor here in Spain. Juan says when he was a little boy, he always dreamed of being a bullfighter and now his dream has come true. For three years, Juan has been practicing in small bull rings, but this summer his manager took him to Bayonne across the border into France.

Bayonne has a big bull ring and thousands of summer tourists go there every year. Juan told Papá that the people at Bayonne get angry if they do not have famous bullfighters and the most important bulls; and if they do not like the bulls they shout things like, "Donkey with horns!" and start throwing things. If they don't think the bull-fighters are very brave, they will shout insults and stamp their feet to make a lot of noise. When the family heard Juan was to fight in the bull ring of Bayonne, we were all afraid, but Juan won all the prizes! Women threw flowers to him and men hurled their hats into the ring! Señor de Gonzáles was so delighted he arranged for Juan to fight the best bull Papá ever raised, last week in Seville.

How I wish I could have seen Juan walk into the ring in his bullfighter's suit! Imagine how magnificent! It is all embroidered in gold and silver thread. Señor de Gonzáles told Papá and Mamá how proud and handsome Juan looked and how excited the people were when Juan proved how brave he was. The newspaper writers say Juan is the new star of the ring! So now, Señor de Gonzáles has invited all his friends, the important managers who hire the bullfighters and the gentlemen who write for the newspapers, to the big fiesta. Mamá and Catalina, Lucretia, Marcelita, and I have much to do to get the fiesta ready. I have helped Mamá cook before, but this is the first time I have cooked for guests and, of course, I have never cooked for such a great occasion.

We have swept the patio of the beautiful *hacienda*, watered the hanging flower baskets, tidied the bird cages, and cleaned the little fountain that makes such a lovely sound. The patio is ready for the long tables and chairs. So now I must hurry to the kitchen because Mamá has given me special dishes of my own to do. I am going to prepare: *Pollo con Mayonesa* (Chicken with Mayonnaise), *Estofado Montanese* (Beef Stew), *Flan con Mermelada de Fresa* (Custard with Strawberry Preserves), and *Pasteles* (delicious little cakes). I am so very happy and excited!

Hasta la vista,
María Teresa

Conchas de Pollo con Mayonesa
CHICKEN SHELLS WITH MAYONNAISE
Serves 6

3 eggs
1 double chicken breast (raw)
  (approximate weight ¾ pound)
1 carrot (approximately 6 inches long)
2 outer celery stalks (leaves, too)
½ cup parsley tops (left whole)
½ teaspoon salt
¼ teaspoon ground, black pepper
3 cups cold water
2 large tomatoes (4 to 5 inches wide)
½ cup coarsely chopped parsley tops
12 slices sweet-sour pickles
½ cup mayonnaise
crisp lettuce leaves
red radishes
finely chopped parsley (for garnishing)

FIRST:
Hard boil 3 eggs in a small pot, peel, and cool according to directions on page 16.

SECOND:
When you buy your double chicken breast, ask the butcher to cut it into two separate breasts. Or, cut it in half along the bone

with poultry shears. Put the 2 pieces in a 9-inch frying pan (with a cover). Peel* 1 carrot and cut into several thick pieces. Carefully wash 2 outer stalks of celery (celery grows in mud and is almost always dirty). Cut each stalk into 3 or 4 pieces and keep the top leaves. Remove and discard the stems from ½ cup of parsley and put the parsley with all the vegetables on top of the chicken. Sprinkle with ½ teaspoon of salt and ¼ teaspoon of pepper. Pour just enough cold water (approximately 3 cups) on top to cover everything and put on the pan cover. Turn the heat up high. When the water starts to boil* reduce the heat to a simmer.* Simmer for 20 minutes altogether. After the first 10 minutes, take a long-handled fork and turn the chicken breasts so they cook on the other side. At the end of 20 minutes, use the long-handled fork to remove the chicken breasts to a breadboard and let them cool.

THIRD:

While the chicken is cooling, slip the skins off 2 large tomatoes. You will need boiling* water for this. (You may use the water in which the chicken was cooked by draining off the vegetables and pouring the hot water into the pot in which you hard-boiled the eggs. Turn up the heat so the water will boil.) One at a time, put the tomatoes into a large slotted kitchen spoon and ease them carefully into boiling water. (Don't dump them in! Remember, boiling water hurts when it splatters.) Leave each tomato in the boiling water for ten seconds. Remove the tomatoes to a little bowl, cover with cold water. After a few moments, remove them from the water, take a paring knife, pull off the skins, and dig out the stem ends. Divide the tomatoes into quarters and scrape the seeds out with a teaspoon. Put the quartered tomatoes on the breadboard and cut them into tiny pieces. Put them in a large bowl. With a pair of scissors, cut up ½ cup of parsley tops (stems removed) into tiny pieces and add to bowl. Cut up the hard-boiled eggs, then chop them with a chopping knife on the bread-board and put the pieces in the bowl. Cut 12 slices of sweet-sour pickles into tiny pieces and add to other ingredients. Remove *all* the bones from the chicken breast and cut the meat into small pieces. Add that to everything else in the bowl. Measure out ½ cup of mayonnaise, put it into the bowl, and mix with a wooden spoon until all the different ingredients are coated with mayonnaise.

FOURTH:

Cover 6 individual serving shells (often used for baking, but if you haven't any shells, salad plates will do) with crisp, freshly rinsed and dried lettuce leaves. Heap the chicken mixture on top of the leaves, and be sure that all the portions are even. Wash and slice several red radishes, and decorate* the tops with slices of radish and a sprinkling of finely chopped parsley. If the salad has to wait, cover with wax paper and refrigerate until ready. Good the next day but better when fresh.

WHAT YOU'LL NEED:

small pot	little bowl
poultry shears	paring knife
9-inch frying pan (with cover)	teaspoon
peeler	large bowl
slicing knife	pair of scissors
measuring spoons	chopper
measuring cup	wooden spoon
long-handled fork	6 individual serving shells
breadboard	or salad plates
large slotted kitchen spoon	

Estofado Montanesa

BEEF STEW

Serves 6

2½ pounds best beef stew meat

⅓ cup flour

2 large onions (4 to 5-inches wide)

¼ cup olive oil

1 10½-ounce can beef consommé (concentrate)

1 can water

2 large carrots

1 bay leaf

1 teaspoon prepared mustard (hot mustard preferred)

1½ teaspoons salt

1 teaspoon ground, black pepper

1 tablespoon cocoa (see note)

½ teaspoon sugar

FIRST:

Cut 2½ pounds of the best beef stew meat into 1-inch pieces on a breadboard. Put ⅓ cup flour on the breadboard and roll the beef in the flour until each piece is well coated. Push the meat to one side to make room for 2 large onions. (Wipe flour off board.) Peel* the onions and slice carefully. Careful of your fingers! When the onions are ready, measure out ¼ cup olive oil. Pour it into a large, (approximately 10 inches) deep frying pan with a cover. Turn the heat on and, when it is hot, use a large kitchen spoon to carefully slip the onion slices into the oil. (If you are careless and dump the onions in, the hot oil is apt to splatter you!) Turn the heat down and fry the onions until they are light gold in color, stirring* and turning them occasionally with a large spoon. Do not let them scorch.* Scorched onions have a nasty, bitter taste. When the onions are a light gold, place the meat in the pan while continuing to cook the onions, letting the pieces of meat cook until they have lost *all* their pink color. When one side is cooked, turn with a wooden spoon or spatula until all sides are dark in color.

SECOND:

While the meat is frying, pour 1 10½-ounce can of beef consommé (concentrate) into a large pot, fill the empty consommé can with water and pour the water into the pot. Stir on high heat until the two liquids are combined. Let it come to a boil*. While you are waiting, peel 2 large carrots and cut into thick slices. When the liquid is boiling, take a look at the meat to be sure it is cooked on all sides. Add the carrots and 1 bay leaf. Pour the liquid over the meat. (Slowly, remember it is boiling hot.) Take a large spoon and stir just a little. Turn down the heat. The meat must not boil. Just let it simmer.* Cover the frying pan and leave it covered for 30 minutes. Be sure you know what time it is when the cover goes on, so you know when the 30 minutes are up. Do not go off and forget it! At the end of 30 minutes, remove the cover and stir in 1 teaspoon of prepared mustard. Stir thoroughly so the mustard is mixed with the sauce. Season with 1½ teaspoons of salt and 1 teaspoon of ground, black pepper. Stir once again to mix in the salt and pepper then cover again and continue to simmer for 1½ hours more.

THIRD:

Mix 1 tablespoon of cocoa and ½ teaspoon of sugar in a little bowl or a 2-cup measuring glass (see note). Gradually stir in 1 cup of gravy, ladled from the meat, stirring constantly to prevent any lumping. Stir until it is smooth and absolutely no lumps remain. Return this to the frying pan and stir carefully until everything is well mixed. If there are any lumps, pour all the gravy into the blendor and give it a whirl. Then return it to the pan and replace the cover and cook for another 10 minutes. Now it is ready. This stew is very good with rice or buttered noodles and is just as good the next day.

Note: If you use an instant cocoa, you may omit the sugar and use 2 tablespoons of cocoa which will make the gravy even darker.

WHAT YOU'LL NEED:

1 slicing knife	wooden spoon or spatula
breadboard	measuring spoons
measuring cup	large pot
peeler	little bowl or 2-cup measuring
large, deep frying pan	glass
(with a cover)	ladle
large kitchen stirring spoon	

Flan con Mermelada de Fresa

CUSTARD WITH STRAWBERRY PRESERVES

Best prepared the day before
Preheat oven* to 350° / Serves 8

3 cups milk
4 eggs
½ cup sugar
¼ teaspoon salt
2 teaspoons vanilla extract
8 heaping teaspoons strawberry preserves
1 box thawed frozen strawberries (optional)

FIRST:

Before starting, turn the oven to 350°. Pour 3 cups of milk into a pot and turn on the heat. Scald* the milk but be sure not to let it boil. While the milk warms (but watch it!) break 4 eggs* into a large mixing bowl. Beat* them hard with a whisk or spoon as though for scrambled eggs. Measure ½ cup sugar, add to the eggs, and beat both together until the sugar no longer feels gritty. Sprinkle in ¼ teaspoon salt and beat some more.

SECOND:

Slowly add the milk to the eggs. Beat with a spoon without stopping until all the milk is added. Add 2 teaspoons of vanilla extract, stirring until well mixed. Sometimes some of the egg sticks to the bottom of the bowl, so scrape the bottom of the bowl with a rubber spatula or the spoon. Take your time and do a careful job. Be sure all the egg is *well mixed* with the milk.

THIRD:

Put 1 heaping teaspoon of strawberry preserves in the bottom of each custard cup. Put an oven pan, large enough to hold the 8 custard cups, on the kitchen counter or table. Put the custard cups in the pan, pour the liquid custard into a pitcher and carefully fill the cups. Carry the pan close to the oven so you will not have far to carry it once you have poured *hot* tap water into the pan. Rinse out the pitcher and fill it with hot tap water. Now pour enough hot water into the pan so the cups stand in at least 1 inch of water. This is how all custards are baked. The water steams the eggs and allows them to cook evenly until smooth and solid. Open the door of the preheated oven and *carefully* lift the pan onto the center rack of the oven. Close the oven door and bake for 50 minutes. At the end of that time stick a small knife or toothpick into the center of one of the custards. If the knife or toothpick comes out clean, the custards are ready to come out. Remove the pan (careful! careful!) to the table or counter with 2 pot holders. Use a pot holder to take the custard cups out of the water bath and let them cool until they are room temperature*, then put them in the refrigerator to chill. They last several days. They may be served as is or with a strawberry sauce (see note page 22). If served with a sauce, it is best to run a knife around the edges of the cups, then invert them on individual serving plates and allow the custards to drop onto the plates.

WHAT YOU'LL NEED:

measuring cup	deep oven pan
medium-size pot	pitcher
large mixing bowl	8 custard cups
whisk or spoon	small knife or toothpick
measuring spoons	2 pot holders
rubber spatula or spoon	8 individual serving plates

Pasteles

LITTLE CAKES

Preheat oven to 375° / Makes 12*

¼ pound butter (1 stick)
vegetable shortening (solid)
¼ cup sugar
2 teaspoons vanilla extract
3 eggs
1 cup plus 1 tablespoon regular flour
1 teaspoon baking powder
12 candied cherries
¾ cup sugar

FIRST:

Take butter out of refrigerator about ½ hour before starting so it will soften. Before starting, turn the oven to 375° and thoroughly grease* bottom and sides of 12 small cupcake pans (2 to 2½-inches wide). This is done by using any vegetable shortening on a folded piece of paper. Be sure the surfaces of the cups are well covered, so the cakes will not stick. When this is done, put ¼ pound butter (1 stick) in the small bowl of the electric mixer with ¼ cup sugar. If you do not have a mixer, cream* with the back of a tablespoon in a bowl. Cream until soft and smooth. Add 2 tablespoons of vanilla extract. Separate 3 eggs* and add the yolks, one at a time. Mix thoroughly. Carefully measure 1 cup plus 1 tablespoon of regular flour into a bowl, adding 1 teaspoon baking powder to the flour. Spoon the flour into the butter mixture, a little at a time until all the flour has been added. (If using the electric mixer, turn to low as you add the flour a little at a time.) Scrape the sides of the mixing bowl with a rubber spatula, pushing any mixture that sticks to the sides down inside the bowl. This mixes everything equally. If using an electric mixer, remove the contents of the small bowl to a larger bowl. Wash and dry the small bowl and the beaters, then put them back in the machine.

SECOND:

Put the 3 egg whites in the small bowl, turn the machine to its highest speed and beat the egg whites until they are stiff and the mixture stands in little peaks like "donkey ears" when you lift the beaters. (This may be done also by beating with a rotary egg beater.) Scrape all the whites out of the bowl with a rubber spatula or large spoon into the big bowl. Using the same spatula or spoon, fold* the whites into the first mixture. Be very gentle! And be sure to get down into the bottom of the bowl, lifting anything that sticks there so the whites are evenly distributed.

Put 1 candied cherry in the bottom of each cupcake pan. Now, take a tablespoon, dip it into the batter and spoon the batter into the prepared cupcake pans. But, be sure not to fill them *too* full. No more than two-thirds full, otherwise the cakes, which will rise in the oven, will slop over the sides and that will not look pretty. Place the filled pans in the middle of the center rack of the pre-heated oven and bake for 20 minutes. At the end of 20 minutes, test one of the cakes by piercing it in the center with a thin testing wire or toothpick. If it comes out clean and the tops are light gold in color, the cakes are done. Remove the pans from the oven, using 2 pot holders, and put on counter or kitchen table. Five minutes later, run a small knife around the outside edge of each cake, all the way down to the bottom of the pan, and carefully remove the cakes from the pans by turning them upside down on wax paper. Put another piece of wax paper on the kitchen table or counter. This will come in handy later, when the cakes are ready to be iced. The wax paper will catch any of the caramel that may drip down. Place 2 cake coolers on top of the wax paper, place all the cakes right side up, on the coolers, and allow them to cool to room temperature.*

THIRD:

While the cakes are cooling, put ¾ cup sugar in a medium-size frying pan, covering the bottom of the pan with a layer of sugar, and turn the heat to moderate. Use a small wooden spoon (a metal spoon gets very hot at this point, unless you use a pot hold-er). Stir* the sugar until it melts in the pan. Continue to rub with the back of the spoon until the sugar turns liquid (there may be a few lumps; press down on them until they melt), and gradually changes color from clear to pale yellow to light brown. When sugar turns this color it is called "caramel." Be careful not to let it turn *too* dark (it will darken very rapidly even from the heat of the pan after you have removed the pan from the fire).

If it turns *too* dark, it will have a bitter taste. Scrape to one side of pan and tilt pan a bit to keep caramel together so it will not harden on bottom of pan. Should it begin to harden, return the pan to fire for just a moment. Spoon caramel on top of each cake, covering the entire top and allowing it to dribble down the sides. Don't worry about any that drops through the cake coolers onto the wax paper. The paper is there to catch any excess and will be thrown away. The caramel will harden as it cools and makes a delicious, crisp topping. But don't taste it before it cools. It will burn your mouth!

WHAT YOU'LL NEED:

paper towel
12 small cupcake pans
measuring cup
electric mixer, egg beater, or
   tablespoon
small knife
measuring spoons
rubber spatula
smallest bowl for mixer

larger bowl
tablespoon
thin wire or toothpick
2 pot holders
wax paper
2 cake coolers
medium-size frying pan
small wooden spoon

·9·
MARIE-LIESEBETH
OF SWITZERLAND

Grüezi:

My name is Marie-Liesebeth. I live in Switzerland, high in the Engadine. The name of our little town in Zuoz. We are not far from St. Moritz, a much larger place. From all over the world people come to St. Moritz for the winter sports. There are many expensive hotels and shops in St. Moritz, but I like Zuoz much better because it is so cozy to live where everyone knows his neighbor, and anyhow, our view of the Alps is just as beautiful and our ski slopes are the best. I wish you could see our fields in summer when they are full of wildflowers. So many, many different kinds, and what fun it is to twine them into garlands for our hair!

My family lives in a *châlet* (that's what we call our mountain homes). In the winter it is almost covered by snow, but in the summer all the châlets are decorated with window boxes filled with red geraniums and white petunias. How bright they look! All the cows in the meadows wear big bells around their necks. There is a lovely "bong! bong! bong!" sound all day. We have goats, too. When the shepherds bring them back to the town square in the evening, each goat knows how to find his own way back to the barn where he belongs.

I live with *Mueti* and *Pappi* and my younger sisters, Ilse and Cecile. We have a family dog, a St. Bernard, whose name is Hans. I like to think that Hans belongs to me, because we were both born on the same day. We are twelve. Isn't it strange that while I am still very young, poor Hans is already old? Once upon a time Hans used to love to climb to the highest meadow, but now he just sits in front of the stove and is sleepy all the time. Pappi smiles when we talk about how lively our old Hans used to be. He says that he understands Hans very well. You see, Pappi used to be a mountain-climbing guide but now he is through climbing mountains, too. Mueti says she is glad because now she doesn't worry that Pappi will fall and break his leg.

So now Pappi has turned our châlet into a lovely lodge for tourists who come to Zuoz to ski. He sells them skis, mittens, hand-knitted scarves and caps, and heavy woolen socks. And lots of other things, too, that tourists like. Things like cuckoo clocks and souvenirs. Pappi has his shop and Mueti has her restaurant. The restaurant was her idea. She gives the skiers lunch. They are always *so* hungry after they've been skiing since the sun came up!

Mueti is a wonderful cook. I hear what the skiers say when they eat her *fontina,* her veal in butter sauce, and her famous apple cake. I'm sure it's true Mueti is the best cook in the Engadine. The last few years I wore the local dress of the Engadine and helped my cousin Anna (she's nineteen) carry the food into the dining room. But this year I've been helping Mueti in the kitchen and maybe, someday, I'll be half as good a cook. I guess I'm a lucky girl to have a mueti who can cook like that.

When I make fontina, I love to watch the cheese start to melt while I stir and stir until it's smooth. Do you think fontina is hard to make? Well, it is not! And how good it tastes when you spear the crusty bread into the melted cheese! I'll tell you how to make a fontina, but how I wish you were here to eat it, after you had been skiing and your tummy is growling with hunger pains and your cheeks are rosy red!

Nowadays, as soon as I come home from school, I always help Mueti in the kitchen (she often leaves me there alone!). Oh, I wish you'd come to Zuoz! I want to show you the mountains, our châlet, Mueti's sunny kitchen, Pappi's shop, Ilse, Cecile, and darling, sleepy Hans! Yesterday, I baked three apple cakes by myself. Today I must bake four more. There are so many tourists!

Uff wiederluege,
Marie-Liesebeth

Swiss Cheese Fontina
Serves 4

crusty French bread (stale)
1 pound *unsliced* Swiss cheese
4 level tablespoons flour
1 tablespoon butter
2 cups milk
½ teaspoon salt
¼ teaspoon ground, black pepper
½ teaspoon nutmeg

FIRST:

Put out the breadboard. Take a bread knife and cut crusty French bread into *thick* slices (about 1 inch thick). Cut these slices into 1-inch cubes. If the bread isn't stale, turn the oven on to 300°, put the bread cubes on a cookie sheet, and leave them in the oven for about half an hour.

SECOND:

Look at your ½ pound piece of *unsliced* Swiss cheese. If there are rinds at either end, trim off and throw them away. Place a piece of wax paper on the breadboard, put a medium-size grater on top and grate* the cheese by rubbing it against the grater. While doing this, lift the grater every now and then to shove aside the grated cheese, making room for more cheese to come. If there is a tiny piece left, don't bother to grate it, you may scrape your knuckles instead. For safety's sake, just pop it into your mouth for a snack! Sprinkle the grated cheese with 1 tablespoon of flour, then lightly lift the grated cheese up and down with your fingers to mix the flour and cheese.

THIRD:

Melt* 1 tablespoon butter in a saucepan or fondue pot. Add 3 level tablespoons flour and blend well. Stir* in 2 cups of milk, a little at a time. When the milk is all added and it has been brought gradually to a boil,* add a pound of grated Swiss cheese, stirring constantly with a *fork* until melted. Add ½ teaspoon salt, ¼ teaspoon pepper, and ½ teaspoon nutmeg. Now the fontina is ready to be eaten and enjoyed. Each guest is to be given a fork (preferably a long-handled fondue fork). He spears a piece of bread and stirs it in the fontina, then he puts it directly into his mouth. It is good to wave it in the air for an instant as it is bound to be very hot.

Note: Before you start to make a fontina, plan to be ready for the moment when you are going to rush the fontina from the stove to the table. This is how: after you have sprinkled the grated cheese with flour, put a chafing dish or electric plate on the table where the fontina is going to be served. Place a basket containing the bread cubes beside it and long-handled forks. What there is left to do in the kitchen takes only a few moments.

WHAT YOU'LL NEED:

breadboard
bread knife
kitchen knife
wax paper
medium-size grater
measuring spoons
medium-size pot (preferably a
   special fondue pot)

measuring cup
stirring fork

For the Finished Fontina:
1 bread basket
long-handled forks (others
   will do)
chafing dish or electric plate

Swiss Cutlets in Butter
Serves 4

8 ½-inch thick slices veal tenderloin
> or

3 ½-inch thick slices leg of veal
½ cup very fine bread crumbs (may be bought in a package)
1 egg
salt
pepper
2 tablespoons butter
1 tablespoon lemon juice
parsley

FIRST:

Ask your butcher to cut 8 ½-inch thick slices of veal tenderloin and have him flatten them with his cleaver until they each measure about ¼ inch thick. If he cannot give you the tenderloin, have him flatten 3 ½-inch thick slices off the leg. These will be much bigger than the tenderloin so you'll be able to cut each into three nice portions. If you do not have a butcher and must get the meat prepackaged from the supermarket, put it on the breadboard and pound it with a wooden pounder until it is ¼ inch thick.

SECOND:

Place ½ cup of very fine bread crumbs on a breadboard. Flatten them evenly with your hand. Break 1 egg* into a soup plate and beat it with a fork until it is well mixed. Take the tip end of a slice of veal in your fingertips, and pull it quickly and lightly through the egg, turn and repeat on the other side. When moistened on both sides, set on top of the bread crumbs, first on one side then on the other. Sprinkle lightly with salt and pepper. If there are crumbs left after the slices have been covered, sprinkle them onto the veal and pat them in.

THIRD:

Melt* 2 tablespoons of butter in a large frying pan. Get it hot but not too hot, or it may burn. Put the veal slices into the butter, brown on one side, sprinkle ½ tablespoon of lemon juice over the slices, turn them to brown on the other side. Then sprinkle with the rest of the lemon juice. When nice and brown, warm* the plates and put the meat on them. Garnish* with parsley and your favorite potatoes.

Note: Cold or hot boiled potatoes cut up into chunks, seasoned with salt and pepper, and fried in butter until they are a light brown make a perfect accompaniment to this Swiss dish. A green salad does, too.

WHAT YOU'LL NEED:

slicing knife
measuring cup
breadboard
soup plate

small fork
large frying pan
measuring spoons

Swiss Apple Cake
Preheat oven* to 350° / Serves 8

1 cup milk

¼ cup farina

¼ pound butter (1 stick) (left out to soften)

½ cup sugar

3 eggs

1 2½-ounce package sliced almonds (without skins)

½ cup seedless raisins

1 teaspoon cinnamon

1 eating apple

1 teaspoon soft butter

2 tablespoons fine bread crumbs

apricot jam

FIRST:

Before starting, turn the oven on to 350°. Heat 1 cup of milk in a medium saucepan but do not boil. Add ¼ cup of farina and stir* without stopping for 3 minutes until the farina is thick and looks like cream of wheat. Use a rubber spatula to scrape the farina into a large mixing bowl, and allow it to cool.

SECOND:

If you have an electric mixer, put ¼ pound (1 stick) of room-temperature* butter in the smaller mixing bowl. Turn on the switch and cream* the butter. Gradually add ½ cup sugar and work the butter and sugar together until they turn smooth and light in color. (If you haven't an electric mixer, rub the butter in a mixing bowl with the back of a wooden spoon, around and around until it's soft and creamy. Slowly add the sugar, continuing to rub until the sugar loses that gritty sound. This is not difficult, it just takes a little longer.)

THIRD:

Separate 3 eggs.* Let the whites drop into a bowl and put the yolks into a cup. Beat* the yolks with a fork and add them to the butter-sugar mixture. Be sure to scrape the cup with a rubber spatula or spoon so nothing is wasted and beat everything together with or without an electric mixer. Either way, mix well, then add the butter, sugar, egg-yolk mixture to the farina, using the rubber spatula again. Beat thoroughly, being sure no lumps are left. (This may be done in the machine, too.)

FOURTH:

Put the contents of a 2½-ounce package of sliced almonds (without skins) into a chopping bowl. Examine them carefully and set 8 of the nicest slices aside to use for decoration* later on. Chop* all the rest until they are very fine. (See note.) Add all the following to the farina mixture: the chopped almonds, ½ cup seedless raisins, and 1 teaspoon of cinnamon. Peel,* core,* and slice 1 large eating apple into thin slices and add that, too. Mix everything together.

FIFTH:

Put 1 teaspoon of butter on a piece of paper towel and grease* the insides of a 9-inch springform or 10-inch oven-proof glass pie plate. Put 2 tablespoons fine bread crumbs into the form, lift it up, tip it from side to side until the crumbs have stuck to the butter on the bottom and sides. If extra crumbs are left, turn the form upside down and gently knock them out. If an oven-proof glass pie plate is used, gently press the bread crumbs onto the sides and bottom of the plate with the back of a spoon. Beat

3 egg whites in the electric mixer (this can also be done by hand with an egg beater) but be sure the beaters are clean and dry. Now beat until the egg whites stand up in peaks like "donkey ears" when you lift the beaters from the mixture. When the whites are ready, fold* them into the mixture. Now spoon lightly into the baking form, using a rubber spatula to scrape the last bit into the prepared form. Place the filled form on the center rack of a preheated 350° oven. In an hour it should be done but, to be certain, test by sticking a toothpick or thin testing wire into the center. If it comes out clean, the cake is done. Use 2 pot holders to carefully remove from the oven. Allow the cake to cool in the form, then remove by opening the ring of the springform and removing ring. The cake may be served and cut on the bottom of the springform but it will look more attractive if a long, thin spatula or knife is used to cut between the cake and the metal bottom, and the cake is gently slid off the metal bottom onto a serving plate. This cake is not too tender so you should not have any trouble transferring it onto the plate. If you use an over-proof glass pie plate, there is no need to transfer the cake. In either case, smear the top with apricot jam, using a spatula. Use no whole pieces, only the runny part. Arrange a pretty daisy in the center with the 8 pieces of almond slices you set aside.

Note: When it comes to chopping the nuts, if you have a blendor put part of the nuts into the machine (not all at one time). Turn it to low. After a moment, turn it off. Turn it on, turn it off. Empty the contents into a small bowl. Repeat and continue in the same way. This will grind the nuts into a fine powder and that is how it should be. If they are not powder-fine, the cake will be heavy. If you do not have a blendor and are going to use a nut grinder, the ground nuts must be put through a sieve into a bowl until the required amount of "powdered nuts" is achieved. Be sure you grind any unpowdered bits over again.

WHAT YOU'LL NEED:

measuring cup

medium saucepan

stirring spoon

rubber spatula

3 mixing bowls (1 large,
    1 medium, 1 small)

electric mixer or wooden spoon

small fork

chopping bowl and chopper,
    or electric blendor

sieve

small bowl

measuring spoons

peeler

apple corer

1 small slicing knife

small pieces of paper towel

spoon

9-inch springform or 10-inch
    oven-proof glass pie plate

thin piece wire or toothpick

2 pot holders

large spatula

serving plate

·10·
BETTY JANE
OF THE U.S.A.

Hi:

My name is Betty Jane and I live in Brooklyn across the river from New York City in New York State in the U. S. A. I love Brooklyn and I wish I knew why people laugh when a comic mentions it. My mother and I live in a brownstone walkup that years ago belonged to a single family. Now it's full of small apartments with lots of families. Our street is nice, with trees that grow out of dirt squares along the edges of the sidewalk. In spring, when the trees are green, I can watch the sparrows build their nests.

My mother is very pretty. We share one small room as a bedroom and we have a living room with a small fireplace. Only there is never any fire, even when it's cold, because my mother says that logs are too hard to find in the city. There's a bathroom with a shower and a tiny, tiny kitchenette. Mom always laughs at it because she says if she didn't wear size 8, we'd never fit in there together!

Mom is really beautiful. Her hair is gold, her eyes are blue, and her mouth looks like a laugh is coming. She's always good to me and, when she has a little extra money, she buys me pretty things like a brand-new sweater or a petticoat with lace. Mom is a model for an elegant store near Fifth Avenue and she works five days a week. Mostly when she comes home at night, after the long subway ride, she's very, very tired so I take good care of her. I rub her neck and shoulders and both her feet, and I tell her everything I've done that day. We tell each other everything. She's told me all about my father who was a pilot (we have his medals in a case) and how he got killed in a plane crash. We have a photograph of him, and I am very glad I have brown eyes like his but wish I had his curly hair!

As I was saying, when Mom comes home at night, she is very, very tired. Mostly we put TV dinners in the oven and eat them on our laps. Mom never really learned to cook and says she doesn't have the time to learn, but she does fix yummy sandwiches or hamburgers or chops on weekends when she has time. Mrs. O'Brian thinks we're starving to death and she wants to change all that. I guess I've been a long time getting to the point because that's what I want to tell you all about.

My best friend, next to Mom, is a girl who's in my class at school. She lives on my street in the building next to ours and she is just my age. Her name is Mary Margaret O'Brian. The O'Brian family have a different kind of house; it's not a brownstone and it's not a brick apartment house. It's a big white house of wood with a chimney on the roof and a porch in front, and I like it very much. Mr. O'Brian is a police lieutenant and he's always jolly. Mrs. O'Brian's name was Katie Shaunessy and she's fat and jolly, too. There are eleven kids in the family — their names are Patrick, Timmy, John, Joe, Mary Margaret, Annie, Sue, and Mamie. The littlest ones are Carrie, Jimmy, and Pete. Whew! I had a hard time learning that! Mr. O'Brian's always hugging everyone and slapping their behinds. Mary Margaret says that's his way of showing that he loves them all.

When school is out, Mary Margaret and I walk over to her house. Mrs. O'Brian's always busy but she doesn't mind, she says. She likes having folks around, especially when she's cooking. "Warm and cozy," she says. She's teaching all her girls to cook. She'd rather cook than breathe, she says. I guess she knew what I was thinking when she said, "Betty Jane, don't just stand there staring, there's nothing better for a woman, even at your age, than rollin' up her sleeves and gettin' busy in the kitchen!" I was going to say how much I'd love to when she said, "Clears the fog away, like the breeze right off the river!" And she laughed and laughed. She's always having so much fun that, even when we don't know what's so funny, we laugh along with her!

I'm glad I'm learning how to cook. I'll be able to help Mom, and maybe soon we won't have frozen dinners, which aren't all that good. I have a big surprise for Mom, and Mrs. O'Brian says I'm doing fine. In two days, it's Mom's birthday, and I'm going to bring her to the O'Brians' house for dinner.

Mrs. O'Brian has already told me what I'm to do. "We'll all sit down to dinner and watch you let the cat out of the bag! You can make an oyster stew, a meat loaf with a good tomato sauce, that Waldorf salad the likes of which you made today, and a grand chocolate birthday cake. And only because you're a beginner, I'll let you use a cake mix.

I'll show you how to fix it so's no one'll know the differ-
ence. But I'm not going to let you get in the habit of using
those contraptions! Next week you'll start a cake from
scratch and no complaining or I'll take the back o' my
hand to you! I've an enormous box of candles, since some-
one's always havin' a birthday in this house but you'll only
use a few to decorate your cake. Your mother won't want
things like candles giving her age away!"

When Mrs. O'Brian says things like that, I always tell
them to Mom to make *her* laugh. But this time I can't because it's Mom's birthday cake. Oh my, there's so much to
think about! So, so long for now.

'Bye,
Betty Jane

Oyster Stew
Serves 4

3 cups milk
1 cup half-and-half or light cream (½ pint)
4 tablespoons butter (½ stick)
oyster liquor (see note 1)
1 pint oysters (see note 1)
½ teaspoon salt
¼ teaspoon ground, black pepper
½ teaspoon celery salt
2 teaspoons freshly chopped parsley

FIRST:

Pour 3 cups of milk and 1 cup half-and-half or light cream into a good-size pot. Heat thoroughly but *do not boil.* At the same time, melt* 4 tablespoons of butter in a good-size frying pan. When the butter is melted but not brown, add the oyster liquor and stir.* Put 1 pint of oysters into the butter mixture in the pan and cook them lightly. Keep the heat between low and medium and be sure not to overcook. Cook only until the edges of the oysters curl. About 5 minutes should be long enough.

SECOND:

If the milk has formed a skin on top, remove it carefully. A table fork is the best thing to use. Pour the oysters into the milk and use a rubber spatula to scrape every bit of the butter and oyster liquor into the pot. Season with ½ teaspoon salt, ¼ teaspoon ground, black pepper, and ½ teaspoon celery salt. Stir gently over medium heat, just long enough to combine all the ingredients.

THIRD:

Warm* the soup bowls or plates. Use a slotted spoon to divide the oysters into even portions in the soup bowls or plates. Then pour the liquid evenly into each bowl. Garnish* the top of each bowl with ½ teaspoon of freshly chopped parsley.

Note 1:   It is best if you are able to buy fresh oysters from your fish man along with the oyster liquor which adds greatly to the flavor of the stew, so be sure you ask him to spoon as much as he will give you into the carton in which he will put your oysters. However, if fresh oysters are not available in your neighborhood, canned oysters will do. Canned oysters come in several size cans. Two 10-ounce cans should be sufficient and be sure to use about *half* the liquor in the cans to heighten the flavor of your stew.

Note 2:   One cup of chopped celery and 1 cup of chopped onions, cooked until limp in 2 tablespoons of butter, may be added to the soup. Some people even like to add 1 cup of whole-kernel corn. If the corn is fresh, you will have to boil it first until the kernels are cooked through. But frozen corn will do very well. Before adding them to the Oyster Stew, follow the directions on the box. The true Oyster Stew is perfectly plain and simple as given in this recipe. The rest is up to you.

WHAT YOU'LL NEED:

measuring cup	rubber spatula
good-size pot	measuring spoons
good-size frying pan	slotted spoon
stirring spoon	4 soup bowls or plates
small fork	

Meat Loaf
Preheat oven* to 375° / Serves 6

3 eggs
1 good-size onion (4 to 5 inches wide)
1½ cups soft bread crumbs (not packaged)
1½ pounds ground beef
½ pound ground pork
1 teaspoon salt
½ teaspoon ground, black pepper
½ cup milk
butter (left out to soften)
1 #300 (approximately 14½-ounce) can tomato sauce
½ teaspoon sugar
freshly chopped parsley (optional)

FIRST:
Boil 3 eggs until hard (see page 16). Peel* and set aside until
ready to use. Now turn on the oven to 375°, then peel,* slice,
and chop* 1 good-size onion and set aside. Cut off the crusts of
fresh white bread. Discard crusts and pull the soft bread into
tiny bits. Put them in a measuring cup and measure out 1½ cups
of these soft bread crumbs. Don't force them down in the cup,
just fill lightly. All these ingredients must be prepared before
you start to mix the meat.

SECOND:
Put 1½ pounds of ground beef and ½ pound of ground pork in
a large mixing bowl. There is nothing more difficult than to try

to work in a bowl that is not large enough! The two meats may be mixed with a spoon. However, there is nothing to compare to your bare hands (provided they are very clean). When the meats are well combined, add the chopped onions and the bread crumbs. Mix again. Add 1 teaspoon of salt and ½ teaspoon of black pepper. Pour in ½ cup of milk and mix thoroughly until the milk has become completely absorbed.

THIRD:

Grease* with butter a metal (8 x 2¾ x 9½) loaf pan (the kind that is used for baking bread). Put half the meat into the pan. Don't squash it down, just pat it lightly. Lay the 3 hard-boiled eggs lengthwise on top of the meat, leaving a little space between each egg. (Later, when the meat loaf is cut, the individual slices will look very pretty with a slice of hard-boiled egg in the center.) Cover the eggs with the rest of the meat. Again, do not squash the meat down. If you like, arrange the meat a little higher down the center and smooth the top of the meat loaf with your hand. Place the loaf pan on the center rack of the preheated 375° oven and bake for 45 minutes. While the meat loaf is in the oven, heat the contents of 1 #300 can of tomato sauce over medium heat. *Don't boil.* Stir* in ½ teaspoon of sugar. This will cut the acidity of the tomatoes and, as a matter of fact, is always a good idea when using tomatoes in any form. Before serving, warm* a sauce boat and put the sauce into it.

FOURTH:

When removing the pan from the oven, use 2 pot holders. Put the pan on the kitchen table or counter and run a knife around all the inside edges before turning out. Warm the serving platter. Turn the meat loaf upside down on a plate large enough to cover the pan, then carefully invert onto a hot serving platter. Serve as soon as possible, with the hot tomato sauce. If you want the loaf to look very pretty, sprinkle the top wih freshly chopped parsley.

WHAT YOU'LL NEED:

egg beater
small mixing bowl
small pot
slicing knife
chopping bowl and chopper
bread knife
measuring cup
large mixing bowl
measuring spoons

loaf pan
wooden spoon
2 pot holders
knife (table knife)
breadboard
platter
plate
sauce boat or serving bowl

Waldorf Salad
Serves 6

1 cup celery hearts (pale yellow inner stalks)
2 large eating apples
juice of ½ lemon
½ cup mayonnaise
salt (optional)
nutmeg (optional)
½ cup walnut meats
6 large freshly rinsed and dried lettuce leaves
6 walnut halves

FIRST:

Chop* enough celery hearts to fill 1 measuring cup. Set aside. Peel* 2 large eating apples. Remove the cores,* then cut the apples into thick slices. Chop the slices rather coarsely. Put the chopped apples and the chopped celery into a mixing bowl.

SECOND:

Sprinkle the apple and celery with the strained juice of half a lemon by squeezing half a lemon in a juicer or by hand through a fine strainer. This will add to the flavor, and keep the apples from turning brown. Add ½ cup of mayonnaise. Mix well with a wooden spoon until everything is combined. A little more mayonnaise may be added and a small amount of salt and nut-meg if you prefer seasoning.

THIRD:

Coarsely chop ½ cup of walnut meat or halves and add them to the salad. Rinse 6 large, fresh lettuce leaves with cold water and dry them gently with a paper towel. Place one leaf on each salad plate and portion out the salad evenly. Decorate* the top of each mound of salad with an unchopped walnut half.

Note: This is the old-fashioned recipe for Waldorf Salad, but there is no rule that says you may not add other tidbits, such as pineapple or cut-up marshmallows.

WHAT YOU'LL NEED:

chopping bowl and chopper	juicer
measuring cup	small strainer
paring knife or apple peeler	wooden spoon
apple corer	paper towel
mixing bowl	6 salad plates

Chocolate Birthday Cake
Preheat oven* to 350° / Serves 10

THE CAKE

1 Devils Food cake mix
2 ounces baking chocolate
   (2 squares bitter chocolate)
½ cup sour cream
1 tablespoon vanilla extract
vegetable shortening
2 tablespoons flour

THE FROSTING

2 eggs
¾ cup sugar
2½ tablespoons cold water
½ teaspoon cream of tartar
pinch salt
1 teaspoon vanilla extract

The Cake

FIRST:

Before starting, turn the oven to 350°, then follow the directions on the box of Devils Food cake mix. Melt* 2 squares of baking chocolate in the top of a double boiler, with water boiling in the bottom. Then add to mix along with ½ cup of sour cream. Stir* in very thoroughly. Add 1 tablespoon of vanilla extract and stir again.

SECOND:

Grease* 2 9-inch layer-cake pans by putting a little vegetable shortening on a small piece of folded paper towel and rubbing the pans evenly. Put 1 tablespoon of flour in each pan. Lift the pans up one at a time and turn them around and around until they are dusted all over the inside with flour. Should there be any flour left, knock it out. With a large kitchen spoon, spoon the batter into the pans and, to be sure that each pan will have the same amount of batter, spoon into one pan first, then into the other. In this way, both cake layers will have the same thickness when baked. Put the pans on the center rack of a preheated 350° oven and bake for 30 to 35 minutes, or until a thin testing wire or toothpick comes out of the centers of the layers perfectly dry and clean.

THIRD:

When the layers are baked, remove them carefully with 2 pot holders and allow the pans to stand for 5 minutes. Then place a wire cake rack over each pan and invert. Place a third cake rack on top of the cake layer, invert again, and remove the top cake rack. Repeat with the second layer. Allow to cool to room temperature.* At least one half hour. *Do not frost until completely cooled.*

The Frosting

FIRST:

Separate two eggs* and put the yolks in the refrigerator to be used in another recipe. Fill the bottom of the double boiler half full of water. Put it on the stove and turn the heat to high. Put the top of the double boiler on the kitchen counter or table and put in the following ingredients: 2 egg whites, ¾ cup sugar, 2½ tablespoons cold water, ½ teaspoon cream of tartar, pinch of salt, and 1 teaspoon vanilla extract. Set the top of the double boiler in the bottom part as soon as the water is boiling.* Turn the heat down a bit and beat* the ingredients, preferably with an electric hand beater or with a rotary egg beater.

SECOND:

Without stopping, beat until the mixture gets very thick, shiny, and stands up in peaks or strong "donkey ears" when you pull the beater out, after beating for about 5 to 7 minutes. Take the top of the double boiler off the stove, set it down on the kitchen table or counter and let the frosting cool. But be sure to scrape excess frosting from beater into pot.

THIRD:

Cut a piece of wax paper as big as the serving platter, cut in half and place the two halves on the platter before putting the first layer on. After you have finished frosting you can pull out the two pieces of wax paper from each side, and you have a lovely clean plate. Put one layer of the cake on the serving platter and spread it with the frosting, using less than half of the mixture. Put the second layer directly on top of it. It is a good idea to stick a metal skewer in the center of the 2 layers (right through to the plate), because this keeps the layers from sliding. Leave it there until the entire cake is frosted and only remove it just before serving. The little hole made by the skewer can easily be spread over, so do not worry about that. After the first layer is frosted, generously spread the top and sides of the cake with the rest of the frosting. A rubber spatula is a good thing to use for this. While doing this, try not to get any bits of chocolate cake mixed up with the frosting. It looks so much prettier if the frosting stays snowy white! If you like coconut, you may sprinkle finely grated coconut on the top and sides of the cake or decorate* it in any other way that suits your taste and imagination. After all, it is your cake, remember, and you are the chef! Nothing left to do now but place the candle holders and the candles.

Note: Just as good the next day. Maybe better. A cake often improves by being allowed to "set."

WHAT YOU'LL NEED:

electric mixer or large spoon
large mixer bowl
measuring cup
measuring spoons
double boiler
paper towel
2 9-inch layer-cake pans
large kitchen spoon
thin testing wire or toothpick

2 pot holders
3 wire cake racks
electric hand beater or
    rotary egg beater
cake plate
wax paper
metal skewer
rubber spatula
candle holders and candles

Glossary

TO BASTE:

Use a pot holder to pull the pan halfway out of the oven. Whether you are using a prepared basting liquid or the juice from the meat, pour a little over the meat and vegetables, if they are being cooked at the same time, with a basting bulb or long-handled spoon. Be sure that the liquid is evenly distributed over the meat and be very careful not to splash yourself. Baste quickly so the oven door doesn't remain open for too long.

TO BEAT:

To lift the contents of a bowl or pot up and down from side to side with a fork or spoon. If your motion is slow, you are beating lightly; if your motion is rapid and hard you are beating heavily.

TO BOIL:

To boil, the liquids in the pot must agitate strongly and form large bubbles that will burst. Large bubbles exploding with steam indicates that the liquid has reached a rolling or hard boil. For a gentler boil, turn the heat down a little.

TO CHOP:

Put whatever you mean to chop in a wooden chopping bowl and cut through it with an up and down motion by using a metal chopper. This operation may be done on a breadboard with a large chopping knife but is much more difficult. A chopping bowl keeps things from skittering all over the place and falling on the floor.

TO CREAM:

This refers principally to butter. Before you start mixing butter with sugar as you do in almost all cakes, the butter must be softened. This is how it is done. First of all, the butter must be left out of the refrigerator long enough to soften. A half hour or hour (depending on the temperature of the kitchen) should be the right time. After that it must be beaten. Preferably in an electric mixer where the beaters will work the butter until it is very soft and creamy. If you do not have an electric beater, the same thing may be accomplished by rubbing the butter in a bowl with the back of a wooden spoon, then beating it with the spoon, so that you have a creamy mass, instead of a hard stick of butter.

TO CURDLE:

Never bring anything to a boil that has raw eggs in it. Eggs will curdle when they boil. This means they will scramble or separate which will spoil the smooth appearance of any dish, especially sauces.

TO DECORATE OR GARNISH:

To make a platter of food or a cake look pretty. To make it attractive by decorating with things such as parsley (if it's meat or fish, etc.) or with chopped nuts, chocolate sprinkles, etc. (if it is a cake) or with whipped cream should it be a dessert. The recipe will tell you what to use.

TO USE EGGS

To break an egg:

Hit the egg sharply against the edge of something firm such as metal, china, or wood. Plastic does not work as well. Grasp the egg in both hands and pull the shell apart gently with your thumbs. Hold it down low over a bowl, cup, or frying pan (depending on how the egg is to be used). Gently allow it to slide out of the shell.

To separate an egg:

When separating eggs, it is most important to have two containers standing by and ready to receive the yolks in one and the whites in the other. First, crack the egg as explained above, then hold the cracked egg over the container intended for the white. Pull the shell apart and allow the white to drop into the container. In order to free the yolk of *all* the white, it may be necessary to gently move the yolk back and forth from one half shell to the other half. This is not difficult, but may require a little practice. If you are not too fussy about getting your hand sticky, you can empty the egg into your hand and let the white drop through your fingers into the container. This does a very good job, but of course, you will have to wash your hands before and after!

To store unused parts of eggs:

If, for instance you are only going to use the yolks and do not immediately need the whites, put the whites in a jar that has a top. That way they will last several weeks in the refrigerator. The top of an egg cup measures one egg white.

On the other hand, if you have leftover egg yolks, put them in a cup or flat container and cover them with a gentle stream of water until you are sure they are airtight. But remember, leftover egg yolks must be used within a day or two as they do not keep nearly as well as whites. When you are ready to use the yolks, slowly pour off the water and let them slip into a slotted spoon. Be very careful here or they will break and run all over the place!

TO FOLD:

When the recipe tells you to "fold" flour or beaten whites of egg into the other contents of a bowl, use an *easy, light* motion from the top to the bottom with a slow, lifting movement until all the ingredients are well combined. Be sure always to use a *very gentle* movement when "folding."

TO GRATE:

Whatever is to be grated should be rubbed against a metal grater. If you are going to grate lemon peel or orange peel or stale bread (to make fine bread crumbs), use the side of the grater with the smallest holes. If you wish to grate coarsely, use the larger grater holes. When you only have a tiny bit left to grate, pop it in your mouth (if it's cheese, for instance) or throw it away. In any case, watch out for your knuckles against the grater!

TO GREASE:

To smear layer-cake tins or an oven pan with vegetable shortening, sometimes even with butter. The best way to do this is with a small piece of kitchen paper towelling folded into a square.

TO MEASURE:

This is a very important part of cooking as measurements must be exactly as given in the recipe. Measuring cups and measuring spoons make this easy for you. But remember that whatever measurement is called for, it means a *level* measurement. So never heap the flour or the sugar high up in the cup or tablespoon! In order to have the measurement *level*, run a knife lightly across the top. That makes it *level*. If the recipe should call for "scant" that means a little *less* than full. Should it call for "heaping" that means a little *more* than full. Some measuring cups have the one-cup measuring line below the top of the cup, so check carefully and fill the cup just to this line.

When salt and pepper are called for, use about ¼ teaspoon pepper for every teaspoon salt.

TO MELT BUTTER WITHOUT BURNING:

The best way to melt butter is to allow it to melt over a low flame, very, very slowly. If there is foam on top of the melted butter this may be carefully removed with a spoon. Butter melted too rapidly will turn brown. If left on the flame too long it will end up a horrible dark brown and there will be nothing to do but throw it away. Remember, easy does it.

TO PEEL:

Onions:

Carefully cut a thin slice off the top of the onion using a small paring knife. Slip the knife under the edge of the onion skin and pull back all the way down to the root end. Go around and around, doing this until all the skin is ready to be cut off at the bottom of the onion.

Potatoes:

Potatoes are best handled with a mechanical potato peeler. Hold the potato in your left hand and the peeler in your right. Press the peeler against the potato and push it away from you. A long sliver of skin will drop off. Keep turning the potato, pushing and peeling until all the slivers of skin are removed. If you are peeling several potatoes at a time, drop each prepared potato into a bowl of cold water, deep enough to keep the potatoes airtight until they are ready to use. This keeps them from turning brown.

Apples and pears:

The potato peeler may be used in the same way when peeling pears and apples. But these fruits, once they are peeled, must be cooked as soon as possible. Otherwise they, too, will turn brown and it ruins their flavor if *they* are put in water. So, work quickly and if they *must* stand a few minutes, be sure to sprinkle them liberally with lemon juice which helps to prevent them from turning brown. Another way to peel apples is to cut them into quarters, skin and all, carefully cutting the skins off each quarter with a small paring knife, removing the cores attached to each quarter as well. Once this is done, slice each quarter apple into a bowl, sprinkling immediately with lemon juice and with sugar. This is a good method when preparing an apple tart or pie. But if you wish to leave the apple whole, an apple corer must be used. Set the apple on a breadboard, plunge the corer into the center top of the apple, press down as far as you can go, and twist the corer in circular fashion. Pull the corer out then push the core out with your finger. This is the best method when baking apples.

TO PREHEAT OVEN:

Turn the oven on to the heat you are told to use in the recipe. Be *sure* the heat you require is reached before you open the oven door. Ask Mother about the timing.

ROOM TEMPERATURE:

To leave cold food or hot food out in the kitchen until the temperature of the food matches the temperature of the kitchen. In other words, it is the same temperature as the room. You will have to learn by experience the amount of time needed, but usually you can allow a minimum of half an hour.

TO SCALD MILK:

To cook milk until it begins to steam and a skin starts to form on top. When this happens, immediately take the pot from the stove and the milk is ready to use. BUT before using it, remove the top skin by moving the points of a fork lightly over the surface.

TO SCORCH:

When the contents of a pot or pan stick to the bottom, they will usually scorch and burn which ruins the food and gives it a bitter, burned flavor. Beware of this at all times. A double boiler with water in the bottom pot is often used to avoid this. The recipe will tell you when to use a double boiler.

SERVING AMOUNTS:

These are approximate. The number of people to be served by a recipe is listed under the title. If you want to serve only half the amount, halve *all* the ingredients. If you want to serve double the amount, multiply *all* the ingredients by two. Here is where arithmetic comes in handy!

TO SIMMER:

When the liquid steams and small bubbles form. This is the best way to cook soups or sauces. But the recipe will tell you whether to boil or to simmer.

TO STIR:

To move the contents of a bowl, pot, or frying pan around and around in a circular motion with a stirring spoon.

TO WARM PLATES, PLATTERS, ETC. TO BE USED FOR SERVING:

Plates, platters, etc. only take a few moments to warm in a pre-heated oven. If you are not using the oven for any other purpose, turn the heat to 150°, put the plates in, and note that it will only take about 10 or 15 minutes to heat them. However, if your oven *is* in use, you will have to pop the plates into the hot oven after you have removed the food that has been prepared. It will only be a minute or two before the plates are well heated. Be sure to use pot holders to remove the plates from the oven since they may be warmer than you think. Always remember that hot food must be served on heated platters and heated plates. This is one sure way of keeping food from cooling off too quickly.

Index

About the Author

Mildred O. Knopf's love of cooking began when she suddenly found herself on an island in Maine with her family. She says, "Never having cooked anything except fudge, I had to take the plunge and soon discovered that cooking is a creative art."

While raising three children, Mrs. Knopf has traveled extensively throughout the world, kept house in more than seven different countries, and entertained constantly with her distinguished husband, producer Edwin Knopf. She has written *The Perfect Hostess Cook Book* (1950), *Cook, My Darling Daughter* (1959), and *The Food of Italy and How to Prepare It* (co-authored with her husband in 1964), in addition to the *Around the World Cookbook for Young People.*

Text set in Bodoni Book
Composed by Lettick Typografic Inc., Bridgeport, Connecticut
Printed by Halliday Lithograph Corporation, West Hanover, Massachusetts
Bound by Economy Bookbinding Corporation, Kearny, New Jersey
Typography by Atha Tehon